TEACHING ECONOMICS IN TROUBLED TIMES

In the Great Recession of 2007–2010, Americans watched their retirement savings erode and the value of their homes decline while the unemployment rate increased and GDP sank. New demands emerged for unprecedented government intervention into the economy. While these changes have a dramatic impact on society at large, they also have serious implications for the content and teaching of economics.

Teaching Economics in Troubled Times is a one-stop collection that helps pre- and in-service social studies teachers to foster an understanding of classic content as well as recent economic developments. Part I offers clear and teachable overviews of the nature of today's complex economic crisis and the corollary changes in teaching economics that flow from revising and updating long-held economic assumptions. Part II provides both detailed best practices for teaching economics in the social studies classroom and frameworks for teaching economics within different contexts including personal finance, entrepreneurship, and history. Part III concludes with effective strategies for teaching at the elementary and secondary school levels based on current research on economic education. From advice on what every economics teacher should know, to tips for best education practices, to investigations into what research tells us about teaching economics, this collection provides a wealth of contextual background and teaching ideas for today's economics and social studies educators. Additional information and resources can be found at the authors' website neweconteaching.com.

Mark C. Schug is Professor Emeritus at the University of Wisconsin–Milwaukee and former Director of the Center for Economic Education.

William C. Wood is Professor of Economics and the Director of the Center for Economic Education at James Madison University.

D0322916

TEACHING ECONOMICS IN TROUBLED TIMES

THEORY AND PRACTICE FOR SECONDARY SOCIAL STUDIES

Edited by
Mark C. Schug and William C. Wood

Routledge
Taylor & Francis Group

NEW YORK AND LONDON

First published 2011
by Routledge
270 Madison Avenue, New York, NY 10016

Simultaneously published in the UK LEEDS TRINITY UNIVERSITY *AL*
by Routledge
2 Park Square, Milton Park, Abingdon, Oxon OX14 4RN

Routledge is an imprint of the Taylor & Francis Group, an informa business

© 2011 Taylor & Francis

The rights of Mark C. Schug and William C. Wood to be identified as authors of the editorial material, and of the authors for their individual chapters, have been asserted in accordance with sections 77 and 78 of the Copyright, Designs and Patents Act 1988.

Typeset in Caslon by Wearset Ltd, Boldon, Tyne and Wear
Printed and bound in the United States of America on acid-free paper by IBT Global

Library of Congress Cataloging in Publication Data
Teaching economics in troubled times : theory and practice for secondary social studies / edited by Mark C. Schug, William C. Wood.
p. cm.
1. Economics–Study and teaching. I. Schug, Mark C. II. Wood, William C., 1952–
HB74.5.T424 2011
330.071'2–dc22   2010034403

ISBN13: 978-0-415-87771-8 (hbk)
ISBN13: 978-0-415-87772-5 (pbk)
ISBN13: 978-0-203-83887-7 (ebk)

Contents

INTRODUCTION
Mark C. Schug and William C. Wood

Are you a new or returning social studies teacher, intrigued or even frightened by recent major changes in the economy? Whatever your level of experience, and whatever your involvement with teaching economics, this book is for you.

To some teachers, the thought of an economics class is a bad dream, the more so since financial markets melted down and ushered in the Great Recession of 2007–2010. Even in good times, many otherwise well prepared social studies teachers balk when it comes to teaching economics. There are many reasons for this. We will name three:

- First, social studies teachers are better prepared in history, government, and geography than they are in economics. This is reasonable given that these courses are nearly universally taught in secondary schools.
- Second, economists often are their own worst pedagogical enemies. College economics courses you took may have included a numbing, encyclopedic coverage of facts, concepts, and graphs. There may have been little hint about which ideas were most important and offered the most powerful explanations.
- Finally, economists often stress the mathematics of the subject. The fact that economics remains a social science—one that should help us understand and predict people's behavior— is sometimes lost among the equations and calculations.

Still, you can be a more successful social studies teacher if you know the basics of how the economy works. In the Great Recession of

2007–2010, Americans watched their retirement savings erode and the value of their homes decline while the unemployment rate increased and GDP sank. New demands emerged for unprecedented government intervention in the economy. We have witnessed extraordinary increases in new government spending, new regulations on business, protectionist legislation, new controls on credit, and demands for tax hikes. These and many other changes have implications for what economics we teach.

Economics also makes important contributions to other social studies courses. A complete understanding of history, for example, requires a careful integration of key concepts and ideas from several of the social sciences. The National Council for History Education (1997, p. 8) states:

> History is indispensible to an ordered view of the natural sciences, the social sciences, and the humanities. In this sense history is the generative subject, through which students gain understanding of, and respect for, human accomplishments in all fields of endeavor.

The NCHE goes on to explain that geography and history are "constant companions." It is nearly impossible to study one without the study of the other. Similar points can be made for military, diplomatic, and religious history. Where is economics in all this? Most often, it is the missing link. For various reasons, the connection between history and economics is rarely made. But, it is nonetheless fundamental. The year 1776, for example, produced not one but two documents of historically significant importance to the new nation. One, of course, was the Declaration of Independence. The other was Adam Smith's *Wealth of Nations*. The founders had read Smith. The ideas of Smith were subsequently imbedded into key parts of the Constitution. As a result, the Constitution established a framework for the efficient conduct of economic affairs. It defined the protection of private property and specified that contracts would be enforced in even-handed fashion; it stipulated rules for bankruptcy, an important element since bankruptcy implies a failure to fulfill contracts. In short, the Constitution created a system of well specified property rights, which reduced uncertainty and permitted the development of free markets—essential, in Adam Smith's view, for a productive economy.

Interest in increasing the amount of economics we teach in social studies is clearly on the rise. Economics has joined history, government, and geography in what's known collectively as the "big four" social studies subjects. More states than ever before now require a course in high school economics for graduation. As a result, enrollments in high school economics courses have been increasing. Economics is included in virtually all state and national social studies standards. Finally, enrollments in economics-related subjects are also on the rise. Personal finance state standards and required high school courses in personal finance are increasing. There has also been a widespread push for increasing amounts of entrepreneurship education.

Overview of the Chapters

The contributors to this book hope to help new and continuing teachers of economics in understanding and teaching classic content as well as recent economic developments. The book itself is divided into three parts. Part I provides a summary of important content and current controversies in the field of economics—content every social studies teacher needs to know. Part II includes suggestions for teaching within different contexts including courses in economics, personal finance, history, and entrepreneurship. Part III concludes with two chapters which summarize research findings for teaching economics at the elementary and secondary school levels.

Part I: The Changing Economic Scene

In good times and bad, there are primary principles of economics that every social studies teacher needs to know. In Chapter 1, James Gwartney and Mark C. Schug explain these principles. They stress how incentives influence people's behavior. They explain that we all face scarcity and, as a result, we have to make choices and those choices involve costs. The authors stress that few choices are "either/or" decisions. Instead, most decisions are made at the margin—where choosers consider the impact of incremental changes. The authors go on to stress the importance of trade and explain how the institutions which protect private property are the key to promoting prosperity. They close with warnings about secondary effects or the unintended consequences of policies which often actually defeat their desired outcome.

In Chapter 2, M. Scott Niederjohn shows how the Great Recession of 2007–2010 reopened a debate on what many economists regarded as more or less settled matters: What should be the primary tools used by the federal government to stabilize the economy? For years, economic policy tended to rely on monetary policy. In the financial crisis of 2007, however, the more activist polices of John Maynard Keynes, policies often associated with the thinking of most economists from the 1930s to the 1970s, were revived. Professor Niederjohn offers clear explanations about the current workings of monetary and fiscal policy.

In Chapter 3, Dwight R. Lee provides new insights into issues related to international trade. The U.S. economy took an historic nose-dive in 2007–2010. It was the worst downturn since the Great Depression. Elected officials and dozens of interest groups called for a "time out" in negotiating new agreements to expand international trade, and others wanted to reduce that trade by canceling existing trade agreements. The stated concern was that trade with countries in which labor costs are much lower than America's forces U.S. workers to either accept lower salaries and wages or lose their jobs to low-paid foreign workers. This concern raises the question—is the goal of free international trade out of date? The author provides clear explanations of elusive economic concepts such as scarcity, absolute advantage and comparative advantage.

In Chapter 4, Angela M. Smith and William C. Wood explain how recent events are best understood by questioning two key implicit assumptions: (1) first, that government regulation is conducted in the public interest by neutral public servants; and (2) that individual consumers operate in a highly rational fashion. Traditional models of government regulation come from identifying market problems such as monopoly or imperfect information and casually assuming that government could easily step in to correct the problems. Better answers come from the methods of public choice, the application of economic analysis to the study of government. Traditional models of individual behavior assume a high degree of rationality. Behavioral economics provides a useful counterweight, showing how people may fail to take actions that are rationally in their best interests. Overconfidence, procrastination, and mis-estimation of risk all interfere with the ability to achieve the best outcomes.

The authors conclude by providing some applications of these principles, including how personal finance education can arm consumers against behavioral traps and how miscalculations of risk have combined with the predictable tendencies of regulators to produce financial market meltdowns.

Perhaps as a result of the recent financial crisis and widespread skepticism regarding the actions of Wall Street bankers, people are often suspicious of markets and regard economics—the study of markets—as somehow tainted. In Chapter 5, J.R. Clark and Mark C. Schug provide insights into the ways that markets may actually promote ethical behavior. Many people have difficulty understanding markets because they suspect that markets are fundamentally immoral. Do markets depend on greed? Is self-interested behavior the same as greed? How do competition and scarcity influence moral behavior? Do people do everything for money? The authors address each of these questions and then explain how markets influence moral behavior including discipline, honesty, trustworthiness, tolerance, cooperation, and courtesy. The authors conclude with suggestions for teaching.

Part II: Making Economics Cool in School

In Chapter 6, Jane S. Lopus enlisted the help of several experienced and highly successful high school economics teachers to offer our readers practical advice on how to get off to a great start teaching high school economics. Among other things, she suggests that teachers stress the economic way of thinking (explained in more detail in Chapter 1). She explains the importance of focusing on standards and provides a sample syllabus. She notes that personal finance has grown in importance and will require attention in a high school economics course. She offers suggestions on using high school and college economics textbooks. She concludes with suggestions for finding great supplemental instructional materials and ways to take advantage of opportunities for professional development.

In Chapter 7, John Morton, a highly experienced teacher of high school economics and of Advanced Placement (AP) economics, explains how such a course offers important and practical benefits to students. He provides practical advice on how to get started teaching AP economics including using web-based resources, preparing a syllabus, obtaining advanced training, and selecting a textbook and supplementary materials. The author goes on to offer specific pedagogical advice including graphing early and often, evaluating often to check for understanding, and providing lots of opportunities for practice.

In Chapter 8, Michael S. Gutter and Selena Garrison explain that now more than ever, financial security is linked to the financial choices consumers make. Consumer behavior today is tracked through credit bureaus and other agencies, impacting the access consumers have to loans, rental property, mobile phones, and insurance; it will also impact the cost. The authors explain how the principles of personal financial education are grounded in economic theory. They note how economics helps to explain savings, consumption, investing, and insurance behaviors. The authors close with several practical suggestions for teaching including sources of personal curriculum materials for classroom use, using case studies, and developing opportunities for service learning.

In Chapter 9, Barbara Flowers explains that although there have always been good reasons to teach entrepreneurship in high school, those reasons have multiplied with recent structural changes in the economy. Few students graduating today can count on steady employment at a single firm to make a career; instead, rapid turnover is more likely. Bright students with a desire to succeed may find entrepreneurship more attractive than working for someone else. But how can they get started? This chapter sets forth principles of high school entrepreneurship education based on experience with the American Dream Youthpreneurship Program in St. Louis.

In Chapter 10, Lucien Ellington explains history as a naturally integrative discipline that frequently draws upon the other social studies and humanities in recreating the past. Economics is one of the subjects that provides important insights into the behavior and institutions of the past. He goes on to present five economics-based case studies of widely studied societies and events usually included in history curricula: Ancient Greece and Rome, Imperial China, Colonial British America, the British Industrial Revolution, and the U.S. Depression of the 1930s. A sixth case study is also included that is intended to facilitate teacher and student comprehension of current economic problems through identifying lessons that can be learned from comparisons of the economic policies of the Great Depression with the Great Recession of 2007–2010. A table containing annotated descriptions of economic history pedagogical resources is also included in the chapter.

Part III: Research Findings in Economic Education

In Chapter 11, Phillip J. VanFossen summarizes research findings regarding teaching economics at the primary (K–3) and intermediate (4–6) grade levels. Numerous studies reveal that children can grasp important economic ideas at young ages. This is important because, like any important subject, economic ideas need to be taught more than once to build understanding. Several exciting programs are used successfully at the middle and elementary grades. The author concludes with a summary of effective approaches for teaching economics at these grade levels including using children's literature, Internet sources, and supplemental curriculum materials.

In Chapter 12, Michael Watts and William B. Walstad place economic education in a historical context, stressing what research tells us about teaching economics at the high school level. They review the long-standing debate among economists about the rationale, feasibility, and appropriate policies for teaching economics at the precollege level. They then provide a summary of research findings in economic education stressing the amount of time students spend on economics in their classes, teachers' knowledge and training in economics and the use of instructional materials with good economics content, and pedagogical methods that students and teachers find interesting and accessible. The authors conclude by summarizing what we know and don't know about teaching economics in high school.

Taken as a whole, these chapters provide insights that will be useful to a variety of new and returning social studies teachers. Economics allows better understanding of the world and promotes better choices by those who learn its lessons. We hope that this book is helpful and we invite you to submit reactions, resources and teaching tips at our companion website: http://neweconteaching.com.

PART I

THE CHANGING ECONOMIC SCENE

1

WHAT EVERY HIGH SCHOOL STUDENT AND TEACHER NEEDS TO KNOW ABOUT ECONOMICS

James Gwartney and Mark C. Schug

In teaching economics to students before college, most often we have only one opportunity to get it right. Most high school students will not go to college. For those that do, only a handful will study economics. American students will have many opportunities to study U.S. history and American government in the K–12 curriculum. However, they will only study economics once—in the high school economics course or perhaps in a related business or social studies course.

We need to get the economic content right the first time around. What economics is most important for high school students to learn? We think the central focus of an introductory course in economics should be teaching students how to think economically. The Great Recession of 2007–2010 underscores the importance of having widespread economic understanding. For example, a better understanding of the credit markets would have contributed to reducing the severity of the financial collapse. Economic thinking should have suggested to lenders and borrowers alike that changes in the rules of lending which, in turn, provided incentives for high risk-taking would almost certainly lead to a collapse. Moreover, widespread economic understanding would have helped citizens to better analyze the policy alternatives that were implemented and those that were not.

In a market economy such as that in the United States, Canada, and other parts of the world, our individual choices largely determine the course of our lives. At the same time, as voters and citizens we make decisions that affect the laws or "rules of the game" that guide these individual choices. To choose intelligently, both for ourselves and for society generally, we must understand some basic principles of human behavior. That is the task of economics—to explain the forces that affect human decision-making.

The following paragraphs introduce ten key elements of economic analysis, ten factors that explain how our economy works. You will learn such things as why prices matter, the true meaning of cost, and how trade furthers prosperity. You don't need a PhD in economics to be able to teach economics well. Most of what high school students need to know is summarized in these ten principles. These principles serve as a starting point for classroom teaching.

1 Incentives Matter

All of economics rests on one simple principle: that *incentives* matter. Altering incentives, the costs and benefits of making specific decisions, alters people's behavior.

Understanding incentives is an extremely powerful tool for understanding why people do the things they do because the impact of incentives can be seen on almost every level, from simple family decision-making to securities markets and international trade.

In fact, markets themselves work because both buyers and sellers change their behavior when incentives change. Prices act as powerful incentives. If buyers want to purchase more of something than sellers are willing (or able) to provide, its price will start to rise. As the price increases, however, sellers will be more willing to voluntarily provide the good or service. Eventually, the higher price will bring the amount demanded and the amount supplied into balance. What happens if it starts out the other way? If prices are too high, suppliers will accumulate inventories and will have to lower prices in order to sell their products. These lower prices will encourage people to buy more—but they will also discourage producers from stepping up production since at the new, lower price the product will be less profitable. Gradually the amount demanded by consumers will once again come into balance with the amount produced by suppliers. This process does not work instantaneously. It takes time for buyers to respond fully to a change in price and for producers to step up or cut back production.

Remember the record nominal high gas prices in the summer of 2008? While a lot of people felt the pain of higher prices at the pump, there was no panic in the streets or lines at the gas pumps. Why? The response of buyers and sellers to changes in gasoline prices illustrates the importance of incentives and the role of time in the adjustment process. In 2008 gasoline prices rose dramatically. In response consumers immediately eliminated unimportant trips and did more carpooling. Gradually, however, they also shifted to smaller, more fuel-efficient cars to reduce their gasoline consumption further. At the same time suppliers of petroleum, the raw material of gasoline, increased their drilling, adopted techniques to recover more oil from existing wells, and intensified their search for new oil fields. In response to market-based incentives, the supply of petroleum, a resource some predicted would be exhausted by 2000, today stands at 1.343 trillion barrels.

Incentives also influence political choices. The person who shops in the mall doesn't behave all that differently from someone who "shops" in the voting booth. In most cases voters are more likely to support political candidates and policies that provide them with personal benefits. They will tend to oppose political options when the personal costs are high compared to the benefits they expect to receive. For example, in a recent poll most Americans favored the idea of expanded health care as long as someone else—the wealthy—paid for it. The same poll found that when asked if they would pay for health care with a tax on all Americans, 75 percent were opposed to expanding health care.

There's no way to get around the importance of incentives. It's part of human nature. For instance, incentives matter just as much under socialism as under capitalism. In the former Soviet Union, managers and employees of glass plants were at one time rewarded according to the tons of sheet glass they produced. Because their revenues depended on the weight of the glass, most factories produced sheet glass so thick that you could hardly see through it. The rules were changed so that the managers were compensated according to the number of square meters of glass they could produce. Under these rules Soviet firms made glass so thin that it broke easily.

Some people think that incentives matter only when people are greedy and selfish. That's wrong. People act for a variety of reasons, some selfish and some charitable. The choices of both the self-centered and the altruistic will be influenced by changes in personal costs and benefits. For example, both the selfish and the altruistic will be more likely to attempt to rescue a child in a three-foot swimming pool than in the rapid currents approaching Niagara Falls. And both are more likely to give a needy person their hand-me-downs rather than their best clothes.

Even though no one would have accused the late Mother Teresa of greediness, her self-interest caused her to respond to incentives, too. When Mother Teresa's organization, the Missionaries of Charity, attempted to open a shelter for the homeless in New York City, the city required expensive (but unneeded) alterations to its building. The organization abandoned the project. This decision did not reflect any change in Mother Teresa's commitment to the poor. Instead, it reflected a change in incentives. When the cost of helping the poor in New York went up, Mother Teresa decided that her resources would do more good elsewhere (Howard, 1994). Changes in incentives influence everyone's choices, regardless of whether we are greedy materialists, compassionate altruists, or somewhere in between.

2 There Is No Such Thing as a Free Lunch

The reality of life on our planet is that productive *resources are limited, while the human desire for goods and services is virtually unlimited.* Would you like to have some new clothes, a luxury boat, or a vacation in the Swiss Alps? How about more time for leisure, recreation, and travel? Do you dream of driving your brand-new Porsche into the driveway of your oceanfront house? Most of us would like to have all of these things and many others! However, we are constrained by the scarcity of resources, including a limited availability of time.

Because we cannot have as much of everything as we would like, we are forced to choose among alternatives. But using resources—time, talent, and objects, both manmade and natural—to accomplish one thing reduces their availability for others. One of the favorite sayings of economists is "There is no such thing as a free lunch." Many restaurants advertise that children eat free—with the purchase of an adult meal. In other words, the meal isn't really free. The patron pays for it in the price of the adult meal. Because there is "no free lunch," we must sacrifice something we value in order to get something else. This sacrifice is the cost we pay for a good or service. Both consumers and producers experience costs with everything we do.

All choices involve a cost. As consumers, the cost of a good helps us balance our desire for a product against our desire for other goods that we could purchase instead. If we do not consider the costs, we will end up using our resources to purchase the wrong things—goods that we do not value as much as other things that we might have bought.

Producers face costs too—the costs of the resources they use to make a product or provide a service. The use of resources such as lumber, steel, and sheet rock to build a new house, for example, diverts resources away from the production of other goods, such as hospitals and schools. When production costs are high, it is because the resources are desired for other purposes as well. When consumers want valued resources used in a different way, they bid up the price of those resources, and producers use fewer of them in existing ways. Producers have a strong incentive to supply goods for as much or more than their production cost, but not for less. This incentive means that producers will tend to supply the goods that consumers value the most.

Of course a good can be provided free to an individual or group if others foot the bill. But this merely shifts the costs; it does not reduce them. Politicians often speak of "free education," "free medical care," or "free housing." This terminology is deceptive. These things are not free. Scarce resources are required to produce each of them. The buildings, labor, and other resources used to produce schooling could, instead, produce more food or recreation or environmental protection or medical care. The cost of the schooling is the value of those goods that must now be given up. Governments may be able to shift costs, but they cannot avoid them.

With the passage of time, people often discover better ways of doing things and improve our knowledge of how to transform scarce resources into desired goods and services. During the last 250 years, we have been able to relax the grip of scarcity and improve our quality of life. This is the result of increased productivity in response to market forces. However, this does not change the fundamental point: we still confront the reality of scarcity. The use of more labor, machines, and natural resources to produce one product forces us to give up other goods that might otherwise have been produced with those resources.

3 Decisions Are Made at the Margin

If we want to get the most out of our resources, we should undertake actions that generate more benefits than costs and refrain from actions that are more costly than they are worth. For example, a family that wants to purchase a home will save for a down payment by working long hours to earn money and by spending less on entertainment and eating out. High school students who want to go to college will spend more time studying and devote less time to video games than they would if they didn't care about college. This weighing of costs and benefits is essential for individuals, businesses, and for society as a whole.

Nearly all choices are made at the margin. That means that they almost always involve additions to, or subtractions from, current conditions, rather than "all-or-nothing" decisions. The word "additional" is a substitute for "marginal." We might ask, "What is the marginal (or additional) cost of producing or purchasing one more unit?" Marginal decisions may involve large or small changes. The "one more unit" could be a new shirt, a new house, a new factory, or even an expenditure of time, as in the case of the high school student choosing among various activities. All these decisions are marginal because they involve additional costs and additional benefits.

We don't make "all-or-nothing" decisions, such as choosing between eating or wearing clothes—dining in the nude so that we can afford food. Instead we choose between having a little more food at the costs of a little less clothing or a little less of something else. In making decisions we don't compare the total value of food and the total value of clothing, but rather we compare their marginal values. A business executive planning to build a new factory will consider whether the marginal benefits of the new factory (for example, additional sales revenues) are greater than the marginal costs (the expense of constructing the new building). If not, the executive and his company are better off without the new factory.

Political actions should also reflect marginal decision-making. One illustration of a political decision is determining how much effort should go into cleaning up pollution. Debates are currently taking place in Washington and across the nation on the best ways to reduce our collective "carbon footprint." If asked how much pollution we should allow, most people would respond "none"—in other words, we should reduce pollution to zero. In the voting booth they might vote that way. But the concept of marginalism reveals that this would be extraordinarily wasteful.

When there is a lot of pollution—so much, say, that we are choking on the air we breathe—the marginal benefit of reducing pollution is very high and is likely to outweigh the marginal cost of that reduction. But as the amount of pollution goes down, so does the marginal benefit—the value of additional reduction. There is still a benefit to an even cleaner atmosphere—for example, we will be able to see distant mountains—but this benefit is not nearly as valuable as saving us from choking. At some point before all pollution disappeared, the marginal benefit of eliminating more pollution would decline to almost zero.

But while the marginal benefit of reducing pollution is going down, the marginal cost is going up and becomes very high before all pollution is eliminated. The marginal cost is the value of other things that have to be sacrificed to reduce pollution a little bit more. The marginal benefit is the value of a little additional improvement in the air. Once the marginal cost of a cleaner atmosphere exceeds the marginal benefit, additional pollution reduction would be wasteful. It would simply not be worth the cost.

To continue with the pollution example, consider the following hypothetical situation. Assume that we know that pollution is doing $100 million worth of damage, and only $1 million is being spent to reduce pollution. Given this information, are we doing too little, or too much, to reduce pollution? Most people would say that we are spending too little. This may be correct, but it doesn't follow from the information given.

The $100 million in damage is total damage, and the $1 million in cost is the total cost of cleanup. To make an informed decision about what to do next, we need to know the marginal benefit of cleanup and the marginal cost of doing so. If spending another $10 on pollution reduction would reduce damage by more than $10, then we should spend more. The marginal benefit exceeds the marginal cost. But if an additional $10 spent on antipollution efforts would reduce damage by only a dollar, additional antipollution spending would be unwise.

A similar confusion over total versus marginal costs and benefits is found in discussions of how funding for medical research should be allocated. An *Associated Press* dispatch reported in 1989 that about $1.3 billion would be spent on AIDS research and prevention, but only $1 billion on heart disease research and prevention. Yet, the article noted, many more people—777,000—were expected to die from heart disease than from AIDS, which would kill 35,000 (*Associated Press*, July 15, 1989). The article seemed to suggest that the nation was spending too much on AIDS compared with heart disease. This may be true, but the data in the *Associated Press* dispatch did not support that position.

The article provided information on total spending and deaths, but told us nothing about the marginal effects of additional spending. AIDS was a new disease in 1989, and, compared to heart disease, it still is. There is much more to learn about AIDS than about heart disease; we are not as far along on the learning curve with AIDS. So the marginal (additional) dollar spent on AIDS research may save more lives than it would if spent on heart disease. We aren't arguing that this is the case. We don't know. But we do know that without information on the marginal impacts of research spending, it is impossible to know how to allocate spending over different diseases to save the most lives.

The concept of marginalism reveals that it is the marginal costs and marginal benefits that are relevant to sound decision-making. If we want to get the most out of our resources, we must undertake only actions that provide marginal benefits that are equal to or greater than marginal costs. Both individuals and nations will be more prosperous when the implications of marginalism are considered.

4 Trade Promotes Economic Progress

The foundation of trade is mutual gain. People agree voluntarily to an exchange because they expect it to improve their well-being. The motivation for trade is summed up in the statement: "If you do something good for me, I will do something good for you." Trade is productive because it permits each trading partner to get more of what he or she wants.

There are three major sources of gains from trade. *First, trade moves goods from people who value them less to people who value them more.* Trade increases the value obtained from goods even though nothing new is produced. When secondhand goods are traded at flea markets, through classified ads, or over the Internet, the exchanges do not increase the quantity of goods available (as new products do). But the trades move products toward people who value them more. Both the buyer and seller gain, or otherwise the exchange would not occur.

People's preferences, knowledge, and goals vary widely. A product that is virtually worthless to one person may be a precious gem to another. A highly technical book on electronics may be worth nothing to an art collector but valued at hundreds of dollars by an engineer. Similarly, a painting that an engineer cares little for may be cherished by an art collector. Voluntary exchange that moves the electronics book to the engineer and the painting to the art collector will increase the benefit derived from both goods. The trade will increase the wealth of both people and also their nation. It is not just the amount of goods and services produced in a nation that determines the nation's wealth, but how those goods and services are allocated.

Second, trade makes larger outputs and consumption levels possible because it allows each of us to specialize more fully in the things that we do best. When people specialize in the production of goods and services that they can provide easily at a low cost, they obtain revenues they can use to trade for goods they cannot produce for themselves. Together, people who specialize this way will produce a larger total quantity of goods and services than they would otherwise—and a combination of goods more varied and more desirable than they could have produced on their own. Economists refer to this principle as the *law of comparative advantage*. This law is universal: it applies to trade among individuals, businesses, regions, and nations.

The law of comparative advantage is just common sense. If someone else is willing to supply you with a product at a lower cost than you can produce it for yourself, it makes sense to trade for it. You can then use your time and resources to produce more of the things for which you are a low-cost producer. For example, even though most doctors might be good at record-keeping and arranging appointments, it is generally in their interest to hire someone to perform these services. The time they spend keeping records is time they could have spent seeing patients. Because the time spent with their patients is worth a lot, they would reduce their earnings if they spent a great deal of time keeping records rather than seeing patients. The relevant issue is not whether doctors are better record-keepers than the assistants they could hire, but how doctors use their time most efficiently.

Third, voluntary exchange makes it possible for firms to achieve lower per-unit costs by adopting mass production methods. Trade makes it possible for business firms to sell their output over a broad market area so they can plan for large outputs and adopt manufacturing processes that take advantage of economies of scale. Such processes often lead to substantially lower per-unit costs and enormous increases in output per worker. Without trade, these gains could not be achieved. Market forces are continuously reallocating production toward low-cost producers (and away from high-cost ones). As a result, open markets tend to allocate goods and resources in ways that maximize the value of the goods and services that are produced.

It is difficult to exaggerate the importance of trade in our modern world. The Founders, having read Adam Smith's *Wealth of Nations*, recognized this early on. By including the commerce clause in the U.S. Constitution (Article 1, Section 8), they helped set the stage for the development of a highly prosperous free trade zone within the United States.

Trade makes it possible for most of us to consume a bundle of goods far beyond what we would be able to produce for ourselves. Can you imagine the difficulty involved in producing your own housing, clothing, and food, to say nothing of computers, television sets, dishwashers, automobiles, and cell phones? People who have these things do so largely because their economies are organized in such a way that individuals can cooperate, specialize, and trade. Countries that impose obstacles to exchange—either domestic or international—reduce the ability of their citizens to achieve more prosperous lives.

5 Transaction Costs Are an Obstacle to Trade

Voluntary exchange promotes cooperation and helps us get more of what we want. However, trade itself is costly. It takes time, effort, and other resources to search out potential trading partners, negotiate trades, and close the sale. Resources spent in this way are called *transaction costs*, and they are an obstacle to the creation of wealth. They limit both our productive capacity and the realization of gains from mutually advantageous trades.

Transaction costs are sometimes high because of physical obstacles, such as oceans, rivers, and mountains, which make it difficult to get products to customers. Investment in roads and improvements in transportation and communications can reduce these transaction costs. In other instances, transaction costs are high because of the lack of information. For example, a young family moves into a new neighborhood. They know no one. They want to find a teenage babysitter to look after their two daughters so they can go out to dinner and a movie. The parents have to try to find that person: the time and energy they spend doing so is part of their transaction costs in finding a babysitter.

Frequently transaction costs are high because of political obstacles, such as taxes, licensing requirements, government regulations, price controls, tariffs, or quotas. But regardless of whether the roadblocks are physical, informational, or political, high transaction costs reduce the potential gains from trade.

People who help others arrange trades and make better choices reduce transaction costs and promote economic progress. Such specialists, sometimes called middlemen, include campus bookstores, real estate agents, stockbrokers, automobile dealers, publishers of classified ads, and a wide variety of merchants.

Often people believe that these middlemen merely increase the price of goods without providing benefits. But once we recognize that transaction costs are an obstacle to trade, we can see the fallacy of this view. People often talk about eliminating the middleman, but they seldom do.

The grocer, for example, is a middleman. (Of course, today's giant supermarket reflects the actions of many people, but together their services are those of a middleman.) Think of the time and effort that would be involved in preparing even a single meal if shoppers had to deal directly with farmers when purchasing vegetables; citrus growers when buying fruit; dairy operators if they wanted butter, milk, or cheese; and ranchers or fishermen if they wanted to serve beef or fish. Grocers make these contacts for consumers, place the items in a convenient selling location, and maintain reliable inventories. The services of grocers and other middlemen reduce transaction costs significantly, making it easier for potential buyers and sellers to realize gains from trade. These services increase the volume of trade and promote economic progress.

6 Profits Direct Businesses Toward Activities That Increase Wealth

The people of a nation will be better off if their resources—their land, their buildings, their people—produce valuable goods and services. At any given time a virtually unlimited number of potential investment projects are under consideration. Some of these investments will increase the value of resources by transforming them into goods and services that increase the satisfaction of consumers. These will promote economic progress. Other investments will reduce the value of resources and reduce economic progress. If we are going to get the most out of the available resources, projects that increase value must be encouraged, while those that use resources less productively must be discouraged.

This is precisely what profits and losses do. Business firms purchase resources (raw materials, intermediate goods, engineering and secretarial services, etc.) and use them to produce goods or services that are sold to consumers. If the sales of the products exceed the costs of all the resources required to produce them, then these firms will make a profit. This means that profits result only if firms produce goods and services that consumers value more than the costs of the resources required for their production.

The value of a product to the consumer is measured by the price the consumer is willing to pay. If the consumer pays more than the production costs, then the decision by the producer to bid the resources away from their alternative uses was a profitable one. Profit is a reward for transforming resources into something of greater value.

In contrast, losses are a penalty imposed on businesses that use up resources without converting them into something more valuable. The losses indicate that the resources would have been better used producing other things.

Suppose it costs a shirt manufacturer $20,000 per month to lease a building, rent the required machines, and purchase the labor, cloth, buttons, and other materials necessary to produce and market 1,000 shirts per month. If the manufacturer sells the 1,000 shirts for $22 each, he receives $22,000 in monthly revenue, or $2,000 in profit. The shirt manufacturer has created wealth—for himself and for the consumer. By their willingness to pay more than the costs of production, his customers reveal that they value the shirts more than they value the resources required for their production. The manufacturer's profit is the reward for turning the resources into more valuable products.

On the other hand, if the shirts cannot be sold for more than $17 each, then the manufacturer will only earn $17,000, losing $3,000 a month. This *loss* occurs because the manufacturer's actions reduced the value of the resources. The shirts—the final product—were worth less to consumers than the resources required for their production. We are not saying that consumers consciously know that the resources used to make the shirts would have been more valuable if converted into some other product. But their choices, taken together, reveal that fact, sending a clear message to the manufacturer.

In a market economy, losses and *business failures* will eventually bring such wasteful activities—producing shirts that sell for less than their cost—to a halt. Losses and business failures will redirect the resources toward the production of other goods that are valued more highly. Thus, even though business failures are often painful for the investors and employees involved, there is a positive side: they release

much per person today as in 1750. Then we solicit their views on the following question: "Why are Americans so much more productive today than 250 years ago?" Think for a moment how you would respond to this question.

Invariably, teachers mention three things: First, today's scientific knowledge and technological abilities are far beyond anything Americans imagined in 1750. Second, we have complex machines and factories, far better roads, and extensive systems of communications. Finally, teachers usually mention that in 1750 individuals and families directly produced most of the items that they consumed, whereas today we typically purchase them from others.

Basically, the teachers provide the correct explanation even if, as is sometimes the case, they have little or no prior knowledge of economics. They recognize the importance of technology, capital, and trade. Their response reinforces our view that economics is the "*science of common sense.*"

We have already highlighted gains from trade and the importance of reducing transaction costs as sources of economic progress. Economic analysis pinpoints three other sources of economic growth: investments in people and machines, improvements in technology, and improvements in economic organization.

First, investments in productive assets (tools and machines, for example) and in the skills of workers (investment in "human capital") enhance our ability to produce goods and services. The two kinds of investment are linked. Workers can produce more if they work with more and better machines. A logger can produce more when working with a chain saw rather than a hand-operated, cross-cut blade. Similarly, a transport worker can haul more with a truck than with a mule and wagon.

Second, improvements in technology (the use of brain power to discover new products and less costly methods of production) spur economic progress. During the last 250 years, the steam engine, followed by the internal combustion engine, electricity, and nuclear power replaced human and animal power as the major source of energy. Automobiles, buses, trains, and airplanes replaced the horse and buggy (and walking) as the chief methods of transportation. Technological improvements continue to change our lifestyles. Consider the impact of CD players, microcomputers, word processors, microwave ovens, video cameras, cell phones, DVDs, by-pass surgery, hip replacements, automobile air conditioners, and even garage door openers. The introduction and development of these products during the last 40 years have vastly changed the way that we work, play, and entertain ourselves, and have improved our well-being.

Third, improvements in economic organization can promote growth. By economic organization we mean the ways that human activities are organized and the rules under which they operate—factors often taken for granted or overlooked. How difficult is it for people to engage in trade and to organize a business? The legal system of a country, to a large extent, determines the answers to these questions, influencing the degree of investment, trade, and economic cooperation. A legal system that protects individuals and their property, enforces contracts fairly, and settles disputes is an essential ingredient for economic progress. Without it, investment will be lacking, trade will be stifled, and the spread of innovative ideas will be retarded.

Investment and improvements in technology do not just happen. They reflect the actions of entrepreneurs, people who take risk in the hope of profit. No one knows what the next innovative breakthrough will be or just which production techniques will reduce costs. Furthermore, entrepreneurial genius is often found in unexpected places. Thus, economic progress depends on a system that allows a very diverse set of people to try their ideas to see if they will pass the market test but also discourages them from squandering resources on unproductive projects.

For this progress to occur, markets must be open so that all are free to try their innovative ideas. In a market economy, entrepreneurs will be able to try out their new product or innovative idea if they can obtain support of a few investors willing to provide the needed financing. Competition must be present to hold entrepreneurs and their investors accountable: their ideas must face the "reality check" of consumers, who will decide whether or not to purchase a product or service at a price above the production cost. Consumers are the ultimate judge and jury. If they do not value an innovative product or service enough to cover its cost, it will not survive in the marketplace.

9 The "Invisible Hand" of Market Prices Directs Buyers and Sellers Toward Activities That Promote the General Welfare

> Every individual is continually exerting himself to find out the most advantageous employment for whatever capital he can command. It is his own advantage, indeed, and not that of the society which he has in view. But the study of his own advantage naturally, or rather necessarily, leads him to prefer that employment which is most advantageous to society … He intends only his own gain, and he is in this, as in many other cases, led by an invisible hand to promote an end which was not part of his intention (Adam Smith, p. 477).

As Adam Smith noted, the remarkable thing about an economy based on private property is that *self-interest* will further the general prosperity of a community or nation. The individual "intends only his own gain" but he is directed by the "invisible hand" of market prices to engage in actions that help others achieve their goals and promote the general prosperity.

The principle of the "*invisible hand*" is difficult for many people to grasp. There is a natural tendency to associate order in a society with centralized planning. Yet Adam Smith contends that pursuing one's own advantage creates an orderly society in which demands are routinely satisfied without a central plan.

This order occurs because market prices coordinate the actions of self-interested individuals when private property and freedom of exchange are present. One statistic—the market price of a particular good or service—provides buyers and sellers with what they need to know to bring their actions into harmony with the actions and preferences of others. Market prices register the choices of millions of consumers, producers, and resource suppliers. They reflect information about consumer preferences, costs, and matters related to timing, location, and circumstances that are well beyond the comprehension of any individual or central-planning authority.

Have you ever thought about why the supermarkets in your community have approximately the right amount of milk, bread, vegetables, and other goods—an amount large enough that the goods are nearly always available but not so large that a lot gets spoiled or wasted? How is it that refrigerators, automobiles, and

CD players, produced at diverse places around the world, are available in your local market in about the quantity that consumers desire? Where is the technical manual for businesses to follow to get this done? Of course, there is no manual. The invisible hand of market prices provides the answer. It directs self-interested individuals into cooperative action and brings their choices into line with each other.

The 1974 Nobel Prize recipient, Friedrich Hayek called the market system a "marvel" because just one indicator, the market price of a commodity, spontaneously carries so much information that it guides buyers and sellers to make decisions that help both obtain what they want (Hayek, 1945).

The market price of a product reflects thousands, even millions, of decisions made around the world by people who don't know what the others are doing. For each commodity or service, the market acts like a giant computer network grinding out an indicator that gives all participants both the information they need and the incentive to act on that information.

Consider the price of apples in the supermarket. This price reflects what consumers are likely to be willing to pay for their next apple but also incorporates the costs that suppliers had to cover to make it available. As a consumer, you will purchase more apples only if the value of each additional apple (its *marginal* value) is worth at least as much to you as the price. If you are willing to pay the price, you value the apples at least as much as other consumers who might have purchased them and at least as much as it cost producers to supply them. And because you are paying for them, you have an incentive to make the wisest possible decision.

But that coordination is only the beginning of the "marvel." Changes are constantly taking place that affect both the value and the cost of apples, and those changes must be communicated to consumers and producers if the desires of consumers and producers are to remain in harmony. Consider what would happen if the citizens of Omaha, Nebraska, initiate a giant Halloween festival that features dunking for apples. They will want more apples than usual. If apple prices do not increase, there will not be enough apples to go around. As people in Omaha (first individuals, then retail outlets, then distributors) express their desire for more apples, the price will go up. The higher price may lead consumers in other cities and states, and perhaps even countries, to reduce their consumption of apples. Without a strong immediate need for apples, they will prefer to eat fewer apples rather than pay more. The result is that outsiders will eat fewer apples, making it possible for Omahans to consume the desired additional apples—at the higher price, which they are willing to pay.

On the supply side, the higher apple prices will make it more profitable for producers to supply more. Attracted by the higher price, suppliers will take more care to avoid spoilage or damage to apples that are stored and shipped. A short-term event such as a Halloween festival will not affect decisions about planting orchards, but a broader increase in consumer interest in apples (perhaps spurred by respected nutritionists who recommend an apple a day) will lead apple growers to increase the size of their orchards.

As apple growers expand production, their actions will increase the value of resources required for the production of apples, such as seedlings, pesticides, and orchard labor. This will draw resources from other activities into the apple-growing industry. As the prices of inputs to apple production go up, more suppliers will be willing to provide them. Over time, these adjustments will expand the future availability of apples. Apple production will increase as long as consumers communicate through prices that they value additional apples more than they value the goods and services that have to be sacrificed to produce the apples.

No individual or central-planning authority could possibly obtain or consider all the information needed for millions of consumers and producers of thousands of different goods and services to coordinate their actions the way markets do. But *market prices contain this information in a distilled form.* They will direct producers and resource suppliers toward production of those things that consumers value most (relative to their costs that is). No one will have to force a farmer to raise apples or tell a construction firm to build houses or convince a furniture manufacturer to produce chairs. When the prices of these and other products indicate that consumers value them as much or more than their production costs, producers seeking personal gain will supply them.

Nor will it be necessary for anyone to remind producers to search for and utilize low-cost methods of production. The invisible hand of market prices will provide them with a strong incentive to seek out the best combination of resources and the most cost-effective production methods. Because lower costs will mean higher profits, each producer will strive to keep costs down and quality up. In fact, competition will virtually force them to do so.

What would Adam Smith's invisible hand have done regarding the financial collapse of 2007–2010? Modern fans of Adam Smith stress the idea that unfettered markets have a tendency to recover more quickly than when government intervenes. The collapse of the housing market is an example. In 2005, interest rates increased. Consequently, the interest rates of Adjusted Rate Mortgages reset at higher levels. Then, home prices collapsed. The default rate on home mortgages increased. Home foreclosures soon followed suit. Government officials scrambled to pass new laws to keep people in their homes but this merely prolonged the suffering. Instead of trying to keep people in their homes they would eventually lose, a less painful policy would have been to let foreclosed homeowners leave their properties and find housing they actually could afford—such as rental apartments. For the most part, that is what happened. Following the foreclosures, bargain hunters swooped into the market. Great buys were made. Slowly but surely, home inventories began to shrink and home prices started to recover. It turns out that free markets and time are the best friends of the economic recovery. Similar developments emerged in other sectors.

In a modern economy, the cooperation that comes from self-interest directed by the invisible hand of market prices is truly amazing. The next time you sit down to a nice dinner think about all the people who helped make it possible. It is unlikely that any of them, from the farmer to the truck driver to the grocer, was motivated by concern that you have an enjoyable meal at the lowest possible cost. Market prices, however, brought their interests into harmony with yours. Farmers who raise the best beef or turkeys receive higher prices, truck drivers and grocers earn more money if their products are delivered fresh and in good condition to the consumer, and so on, always pursuing the low-cost means to do so. Literally tens of thousands of people, most of whom we will never meet, make contributions that help each of us consume a bundle of goods that is far beyond what we could produce for ourselves. Moreover, the invisible hand of market prices works so quietly and automatically that the order, cooperation among strangers, and vast array of goods available to modern consumers are largely taken for granted. Thus, many fail to either understand or appreciate the wonders generated by the invisible hand.

10 Too Often Long-Term Consequences, or the Secondary Effects, of an Action Are Ignored

Henry Hazlitt, a popular writer about economics during the last century, authored the classic book *Economics in One Lesson* (1979). Hazlitt's one lesson was that when analyzing an economic proposal, a person: "must trace not merely the immediate result but the results in the long run, not merely the primary consequences but the secondary consequences, and not merely the effects on some special group but the effects on everyone" (p. 103). Hazlitt believed that failure to apply this lesson was the most common source of economic error.

Especially in politics there is a tendency to stress the *short-term benefits* of a policy while completely ignoring the *longer-term consequences*. In politics we hear an endless pleading for proposals to help specific industries, regions, or groups without consideration given to their impact on the broader community, including taxpayers and consumers.

Much of this is deliberate. When seeking political favors, interest groups and their hired representatives, lobbyists, have an incentive to put the best spin on their case. They will exaggerate the benefits (most of which they will capture if the policy is enacted) and minimize the costs (most of which will be borne by others). Such interest groups are most effective if the benefits are immediate and easily visible to the voter, but the costs are less visible and mostly in the future. Under these conditions, interest groups can often mislead voters.

Thus voters often authorize actions that they would probably have rejected if they had understood the *secondary effects* or long-range consequences. Consider the case of rent controls imposed on apartments. Cities such as Berkeley and Santa Monica, California, as well as New York City have adopted such controls, usually in response to claims that rent controls will keep rents from rising and make housing more affordable for the poor.

Yes, this is true in the short run, but there will be secondary effects. First, the market for apartments will stagnate. Existing apartments will not be transferred to those who want them most. It will be expensive for someone to give up a rent-controlled apartment, even if another apartment is closer to work, and it will be hard to find a closer one because others are holding onto theirs at the below-market rent.

The lower rental prices will also reduce investments in new housing. Although rent control may force current owners to accept a lower return, this will not be true for potential future owners. Because people respond to incentives, investors who would have put their funds into new apartments will channel them elsewhere. The number of rental units in the future will decline, making it more difficult to find an apartment. Shortages will develop. The quality of rental housing will also fall with the passage of time because landlords receive little in return for maintained units.

These secondary effects, however, will not be immediately observable. When the decline in the quality and quantity of apartments appears, many people will be puzzled about the cause. Thus, rent controls command substantial popularity, even though a declining supply of rental housing, poor maintenance, and shortages are the inevitable results. In the words of Swedish economist Assar Lindbeck (1972): "In many cases rent control appears to be the most efficient technique presently known to destroy a city, except for bombing" (p. 39).

Similarly, proponents of tariffs and quotas on foreign products almost always ignore the secondary effects of their policies. By limiting the importation of products from foreign countries, tariffs and quotas may initially protect the U.S. workers who make comparable products at a higher cost. But there will be secondary consequences, perhaps severe ones.

The steel import quotas imposed by the Bush administration in 2002 vividly illustrate this point. The quotas sharply reduced steel imports, and this reduction in supply pushed U.S. steel prices upward by about 30 percent. At the higher prices, the domestic producers of steel expanded both output and employment. But, what about the secondary effects? The higher steel prices also made it more expensive to produce goods that contain a lot of steel, such as trucks, automobiles, and heavy appliances. American producers of these commodities were harmed by the quotas and often forced to lay off workers. American steel container producers, which had previously dominated the world market, sharply curtailed their employment because they were unable to compete with foreign firms purchasing steel at much lower prices.

Furthermore, there was an additional secondary effect. Because foreigners sold less steel in the U.S. market, they acquired fewer dollars with which to import American-made goods. Therefore, U.S. exports fell as a result of the import restrictions.

Once the secondary effects are considered, the impact on employment is clear: trade restrictions do not create jobs; they reshuffle them. Employment may expand in industries shielded by quotas and tariffs, but it will contract in other industries, particularly export industries. The popularity of the restrictions is not surprising because the jobs of the people actually working in a shielded industry, steel in this case, are highly visible, while the secondary effects—the lost jobs in other industries—are less visible and difficult to trace back to the trade restrictions. Thus many people fall for the "protecting jobs" argument even though it is clearly fallacious when examined more closely.

Government spending also generates secondary effects that are often ignored. Politicians like to argue that government spending on favored projects expands employment. Of course there may be good reasons for government expenditures on roads, increased police protection, administration of justice, and so forth. The creation of jobs, however, is not one of them.

Suppose the government spends $50 billion on a project employing one million workers to build a high-speed train linking Los Angeles and Las Vegas. How many jobs will the project create? Once the secondary effects are considered, the answer is none.

The reason is that the government must use either taxes or debt to finance the project. Taxes of $50 billion will reduce consumer spending and private savings, and this reduction will destroy as many jobs as the government spending will create. Alternatively, if the project is financed by debt, the borrowing will lead to higher interest rates and taxes to cover interest payments. This will divert funds away from other projects, both private and public.

The one million new jobs grabs the headlines, but the loss of jobs in thousands of locations goes unrecognized. As in the case of trade restrictions, the result of this project is job rearrangement, not job creation. This fact does not necessarily mean that the project should not be undertaken. But it does mean that the justification for the project must come from evidence that the benefits are greater than the costs of the opportunities that must be given up if the project is undertaken.

Secondary effects are not just a problem for governments and politicians. They can also lead to unanticipated outcomes for individuals. The recent experience of a first-grade teacher in West Virginia illustrates this point. Her students were constantly losing their pencils; so she reasoned that if she paid them 10 cents for the stub they would respond to the incentive to hang on to the pencil until it was all used. To her dismay, the students soon formed long lines at the pencil sharpener, creating stubs just as fast as she could pay for them. It pays to be alert for unintended consequences!

Conclusion

Economics involves the study of people and the choices they make in response to incentives. As observers of human behavior, economists do not gloss over or take for granted what might seem mundane to others. Market economies have produced a standard of living unimaginable to our ancestors. People of modest means have dwellings with several rooms, electricity, indoor plumbing, furnaces, air conditioners, microwave ovens, refrigerators, televisions, and electronic devices that speed communications to friends, family, and business associates and provide nearly unlimited access to entertainment.

Teachers can help young people understand the world in which we live by introducing them to the economic way of thinking. A few relatively simple but powerful concepts—incentives, scarcity, marginal decisions, trade, transaction costs and profits—provide the core for the economic way of thinking. Moreover, the understanding of students is deepened when they grasp the idea that helping others provides the source for earnings. The rules of the game are also basic to market systems as we strive to establish sound economic institutions and allow the invisible hand to guide most economic decisions. Equally important, students need to understand the potential impact of secondary effects. Failure to recognize the secondary effects has been, and continues to be, a major source of economic error. Thus, it is important to alert students to this danger and the mischief that it generates.

Acknowledgements

From: *Common Sense Economics*, by D. Gwartney, Richard L. Stroup, and Dwight R. Lee, ©2005 by the authors and reprinted by permission of St. Martin's Press, LLC.

References

Hayek, F.A. (1945) The Use of Knowledge in Society. *American Economic Review* 35 (4), 519–530.
Hazlitt, H. (1979) *Economics in One Lesson*. New Rochelle: Arlington House.
Howard, P.K. (1994) *The Death of Common Sense*. New York: Random House.
Lindbeck, A. (1970) *The Political Economy of the New Left*. New York: Harper & Row.
Smith, A. (1976) *An Inquiry into the Nature and Causes of the Wealth of Nations*, Cannan's ed. Chicago: University of Chicago Press.

2

JOHN MAYNARD KEYNES

Dead But Not Forgotten

M. Scott Niederjohn

Introduction

Prior to the Great Depression the vast majority of economists subscribed to a classical economic theory when analyzing the macroeconomy. Classical economists profess a laissez-faire philosophy centered on the idea that while economies go through unfortunate periods of downturn—indeed, many such downturns occurred in Europe and the United States during the nineteenth century—they will eventually self-correct. Classical economists of this time believed that government policies to "fine tune" the economy were counterproductive and, in contrast, they taught that the government's primary role was to maintain a balanced budget and allow the "invisible hand" of markets—which Adam Smith made popular in the late eighteenth century—to work.

The Great Depression led to a profound shift in economists' thinking about macroeconomic issues. As economies worldwide found their self-correcting mechanisms stalled during the 1930s, many thinkers began to question the wisdom of the classical theory. New theories, propagated by John Maynard Keynes and his 1936 book *The General Theory of Employment, Interest and Money*, presented a theoretical justification for activist fiscal and monetary policy during times of recession. Keynesians argued for increases in government spending and tax cuts to counteract the decline in aggregate demand that occurs during recessions due to decreases in household consumption and business investment. Keynesian theories remained popular, and the subject of much academic research and debate, for many years following the Great Depression. However in the 1970s, as the U.S. economy suffered from a different type of affliction—one centered on the supply side rather than the demand side—Keynesian theories experienced decline in popularity. This eventually led to widespread agreement among economists in recent years that the usefulness of discretionary fiscal policy was outdated and that monetary policy was the more effective and appropriate way to attempt to deal with economic downturns.

Debates over how to promote a healthy economy are once again in style, after decades when it seemed the debates were over. The market meltdown of 2008 ended a long string of years in which monetary policy reigned supreme. The Keynesians have made a resurgence in the economic policy debate; however, not without serious critics. Which macroeconomic policy tools will be in vogue in the next 20 years? That's an interesting question without a clear answer.

Monetary Policy Defined

Monetary policy is the regulation of the money supply and interest rates in an effort to influence economic activity including economic growth, inflation, and employment (McEachern, 2007). In the United States, monetary policy is conducted by the Federal Reserve, the nation's central bank, primarily through their control over the federal funds rate. Monetary policies are demand-side policies; that is, they work by stimulating or discouraging spending on goods and services.

A 1977 amendment to the Federal Reserve Act gave the Fed responsibility for pursuing a number of goals for the nation's economy. Essentially, this Act states that the Fed should promote high employment, stable prices, and sustainable economic growth. The Fed cannot guarantee that everyone has a job or that inflation remains under control; this is determined by the decisions of millions of firms and households interacting in the economy. However, the Fed can help create an environment where these goals are more likely to be achieved. How does the Fed do this? The answer is through the setting of the nation's money supply. The Fed does this primarily through three tools, outlined below.

Open Market Operations

The most important, and frequently used, tool of monetary policy is open market operations. At least eight times per year, the Federal Open Market Committee (FOMC) meets to set interest rates. These meetings receive significant attention from many, including the media, with post-meeting reports typically stating that the Fed "lowered interest rates," "raised interest rates," or "didn't change interest rates." Open market operations are the tool the Fed uses to make these interest rate changes.

The Fed uses open market operations to control the federal funds rate—the interest rate that banks charge each other to borrow overnight in the Federal Funds Market. While this may sound complicated, it really isn't. Banks are subject to a reserve requirement mandated by the Fed. Let's assume that banks are required to keep 10 percent of their checking deposits in reserve. Sometimes banks may either fall short of their required reserves or have excess reserves at the end of the day. When this happens, those banks with extra funds can lend them to banks that are short in the Federal Funds Market—where the borrower pays the federal funds rate.

The Fed influences this interest rate by buying and selling government bonds. When the Fed wants to lower interest rates, and encourage firms and individuals to borrow, stimulating aggregate demand, they buy government bonds from securities dealers. In return for these bonds, the Fed credits these dealers' bank accounts at the Fed. This puts more money into the banking system and places downward pressure on the federal funds rate (increases the supply of money). Other interest rates in the economy then follow (like interest rates on car loans or homes) and borrowing becomes cheaper. This is typically done when the Fed is worried about the economy slipping into recession. The hope is that lower interest rates will encourage borrowing and keep the economy strong. On the other hand, the Fed can raise the federal funds rate by selling government bonds. By doing so, they take money from banks (lower the supply of money) and consequently raise interest rates. This is typically done when the Fed fears inflation. They are hoping to slow spending on goods and services by raising the costs of borrowing money.

Reserve Requirements

As we have just discussed, the Fed sets a percentage of checking deposits that banks must hold in reserves. When the reserve requirement is lowered, banks are required to keep less money in reserves, and more money is created in the lending process. In other words, less money sits in bank vaults and more is in the hands of the public to use to purchase goods and services. Conversely, if the reserve requirement were raised, banks would have to keep more money in reserves and less money would be created in the lending process. Reserve requirements are infrequently changed by the Fed, primarily because of the impact that changes in this tool would have on banks and their costs of doing business.

Discount Policy

The final tool of monetary policy that the Fed can wield is called discount policy. Discount policy means changing the discount rate—or the rate member banks must pay to borrow money from the Fed. By lowering this discount rate, the Fed can encourage borrowing or they can raise the discount rate and discourage borrowing. In either case, the money supply is affected. The discount rate is typically changed in conjunction with the federal funds rate. In the recent past discount loans were very rare; in fact, banks shunned them for fear that such a loan might worry their customers about their financial health. However, during the recent financial crisis discount loans were made in record numbers to help save failing banks and financial institutions.

The Fed and the Financial Crisis

During the recent financial crisis that began in 2008 the Federal Reserve took extraordinary steps to support the banking system and help the financial system avoid catastrophe. The Fed reduced its target federal funds rate—through open market operations—to essentially zero percent in December of 2008 and has left the rate at this level ever since. The Fed also increased its balance sheet significantly beginning in the fall of 2008. This reflected the Fed's efforts to make discount loans to—and purchase the toxic assets of—ailing financial firms like AIG and Bear Stearns in an effort to support the financial system and prevent a collapse. Further, the Fed has taken unprecedented actions during the crisis to ensure liquidity, including the purchase of long-term treasury securities and debt issued by the mortgage giants Fannie Mae and Freddie Mac and the purchase of mortgage-backed securities.

The Fed and the Great Depression

The Fed Chairman, Ben Bernanke, is a student of Great Depression history himself. In his 2000 book, *Essays on the Great Depression*, he referred to the Great Depression as the "Holy Grail of macroeconomics." In the Preface of this book, he wrote:

> I guess I am a Great Depression buff, the way some people are Civil War buffs. I don't know why there aren't more Depression buffs. The Depression was an incredibly dramatic episode—an era of stock market crashes, bread lines, bank runs, and wild currency speculation, with the storm clouds of war gathering ominously in the background all the while (Bernanke, 2000, p. vii).

Between 1929 and 1933, the output produced in the U.S. plummeted by almost 30 percent. Further, the unemployment rate surged to over 25 percent and more than 9,700 American banks failed. The number of bank panics occurring during this period was unprecedented, and spurred President Roosevelt to make his famous statement, "The only thing we have to fear is fear itself." The reasons for the onset of the Great Depression, causing unparalleled economic misery in the United States and around the world, have been widely debated.

Unlike the Fed's conduct during the recent financial crisis, it remained remarkably passive during the onset of the Great Depression. The Fed refused to perform its function as a lender of last resort (one of the major reasons for forming the Fed in 1913) for failing banks. The Board of Governors did not fully understand the negative impact that bank failures would have on the money supply and the economy in general. Milton Friedman and Anna Jacobson Schwartz (1963) discussed this in their influential book, *A Monetary History of the United States, 1867–1960*, reporting that the Fed "tended to regard bank failures as regrettable consequences of bank management or bad banking practices, or as inevitable reactions to prior speculative excesses, or as a consequence but hardly a cause of the financial and economic collapse in process." Further, Friedman and Schwartz note that bank failures were concentrated among smaller banks while the Fed was controlled by big city bankers that "deplored the existence" of the smaller banks.

In addition, the Federal Reserve System raised interest rates in 1931 in an effort to support the U.S. dollar; this discouraged business borrowing and caused the money supply to shrink further. With so much less money to go around, businesses could not get the loans they needed and were forced to stop investing.

What does Bernanke make of all this? He fully acknowledges the failings of the Federal Reserve System during the Great Depression. In fact, at a 2002 conference honoring Friedman's ninetieth birthday, Bernanke, then a Fed governor, told Friedman, "Regarding the Great Depression. You're right, we did it. We're very sorry. But thanks to you, we won't do it again" (Ip, 2005). The Fed's response to more recent financial crises, like the October 1987 stock market crash, the attacks of September 11th, and the recent financial panic of 2008, suggests they have learned their lesson from the Great Depression and will take all steps available to them to make sure such an event doesn't happen again.

Fiscal Policy Defined

Fiscal policy, on the other hand, refers to use of government spending and taxation to influence the economy (Weil, 2008). As the government determines how much goods and services to purchase, transfer payments to distribute, and taxes to collect it is engaging in fiscal policy. Increases in government spending and tax cuts are termed "expansionary," while the converse is referred to as "contractionary." Some fiscal policy instruments act as automatic stabilizers while others are termed discretionary. Automatic stabilizers refer to programs that automatically—that is, as part of the normal budget cycle and without action by Congress—expand the economy during recessions and contract it during expansions. Unemployment insurance is one such program. The government collects this benefit in the form of taxes during times of growth and distributes the money during recessions in an effort to dampen the effect of unemployment. The income tax system is another automatic stabilizer program as taxes are collected in proportion to the income and profits earned. More taxes are collected during boom times and less during recessions, acting to slow the economy during good times and stimulate it in the down times.

Discretionary fiscal policy, on the other hand, represents changes in government spending or taxation policy in response to economic conditions. The Keynesian theory advocated discretionary fiscal policy as a solution to the Great Depression. Keynes taught that economic downturns are caused by inadequate total or aggregate demand. His prescription to solve this economic affliction was for government to provide the demand the private sector wouldn't, even if that would require deficit spending. The New Deal programs undertaken during the Franklin Roosevelt administration were direct offshoots of Keynes' influence.

Fiscal policy relies on a multiplier effect to influence aggregate demand. That is, when the government buys goods and services from a firm, or cuts taxes, the policy may affect the economy in multiple ways. Consider the government purchase. Initially this purchase raises employment and profits at the firm directly. Next, as employees of this firm see higher wages and the owners more profits, they respond by spending some of this new income. This leads to more demand for goods and services. This process continues over and over again, hence the name multiplier effect. Thus the multiplier theory states that each one dollar spent by the government can raise aggregate demand for goods and services by more than one dollar. Under the Keynesian theory the size of this multiplier is determined by the marginal propensity to consume or the fraction of this new income people choose to consume rather than save.

A tax cut works in a similar fashion according to the Keynesian theory. A tax cut stimulates spending; again, subject to the marginal propensity to consume. This spending creates jobs and income for

allocations of capital. However, government projects are not subject to such a test—leaving little reason to think governments will be more successful at choosing the *best* projects to undertake than the private sector would be. In fact, given the hurried nature in which these decisions were made, it's likely many of the choices made will turn out to be wasteful pork barrel projects chosen for their political, rather than economic, benefits. If bridge-to-nowhere-style infrastructure projects are funded, we can expect the multiplier estimated by the authors of the stimulus plan to be too high.

Estimating the employment effect. The Obama economic team estimates that its preferred stimulus package will create or save more than 3.7 million jobs. Such a result requires that the spending programs in the stimulus package primarily target and utilize unemployed workers. More likely—particularly in areas like health and energy—jobs will simply move from one productive activity to another in response to the new government spending. Creating projects that specifically target the skills and abilities of the unemployed is a nearly impossible task; suggesting that the net job creation from the plan may be significantly lower than advertised.

Deficit spending effects. A common weakness of any tax cut or spending increase, whether advocated by Keynesians, monetarists, or supply-siders, is that it will increase government borrowing. That debt ultimately must be paid back. If government borrowing is excessive, at some point we will encounter a mix of high inflation, higher interest rates, higher taxes, and dollar devaluation. As Figure 2.1 illustrates, the U.S. federal debt, as a percentage of GDP, is forecast to grow substantially in the coming years. As the chart indicates, it's expected that debt will surpass 100 percent of GDP (total U.S. production or income) by 2011. This represents the highest level of debt, as a percentage of GDP, since the massive spending years during World War II when debt reached almost 122 percent of GDP.

The Supply Side

When it comes to stimulating an economy, discretionary fiscal and monetary policy aren't the only games in town. Economists subscribe to a host of other theories including supply-side economics.

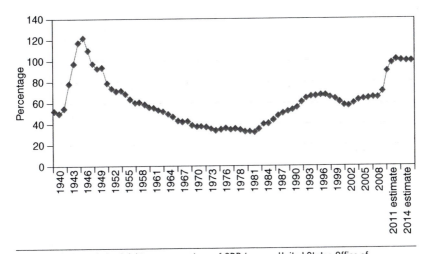

Figure 2.1 Gross federal debt as a percentage of GDP (source: United States Office of Management and Budget).

Monetary and fiscal policies are both "demand-side" prescriptions. That is, they work to increase aggregate demand during times of recession. Such increases in aggregate demand then lead to increases in employment and income, eventually bringing the country back to an era of economic growth. Monetary policy attempts to accomplish this goal by increasing the supply of money and credit. This, in turn, leads to lower interest rates which provide an incentive for consumers and businesses to increase consumption and investment leading to an increase in demand. Fiscal policy endeavors to influence aggregate demand more directly. Such policies add to spending directly either through increases in government expenditures or through tax cuts to households.

Even as Keynesians and monetarists have debated how to increase aggregate demand, supply-side economists and their political allies have been insisting that demand is typically not the problem. They believe that conventional policies increasing spending will only give small upward bumps to the economy. They recognize that influencing aggregate demand is a short-term solution. If a policy can instead stimulate the supply side—that is, the economy's ability to produce real goods and services—a long-term increase in the standard of living is possible. Supply-side economics is a theory that describes how tax rates influence economic activity (Gwartney,

2008). The supply-side cure, therefore, is tax cuts designed to increase productivity, entrepreneurship, and risk-taking. The resulting increase in aggregate supply, they believe, will lead to economic recovery.

To supply-siders, not all tax cuts are equally good. They place their emphasis on the "marginal tax rate," the percentage taxed away from an extra dollar of income earned. A marginal tax rate of 40 percent, for example, would mean that 40 cents of each additional dollar of income would be taxed away, leaving an after-tax reward of 60 cents for the person who earned the dollar. High marginal tax rates kill economic initiative, they believe, and tax cuts that leave marginal tax rates high are useless. As an example, a fixed $500 tax credit to everyone would not affect the after-tax reward of earning an additional dollar of income. It would leave marginal tax rates unaffected and therefore would have no direct effect on promoting aggregate supply.

Supply-siders have pointed to economic results following the Reagan and Bush tax cuts as evidence of success. Advocates of monetary policy cite the accomplishments of the Fed under former chairman Alan Greenspan in the early 2000s as evidence that monetary policy could keep an economy from faltering, even under the stresses of 9/11 and its aftermath. Now Greenspan is faulted for allowing money to grow too much, inadvertently promoting the easy-money rise of housing prices, followed by the collapse that brought on the current difficulties. Perhaps such failures have led to the resurgence in Keynesian-style fiscal policy.

Conclusion

The recent financial crisis has re-energized the discretionary fiscal policy theory first advocated by John Maynard Keynes during the Great Depression. This type of macroeconomic fine-tuning instrument had long fallen out of favor with mainstream economists. While the use of such a policy presents clear challenges, there are weaknesses in every proposed cure to the economy's current troubles. Monetary policy has been pursued and seems to be at its limits; supply-side tax cuts are uncertain in their impact; Keynesian fiscal stimulus seems likely to have some positive impact in the short run but has important drawbacks. The debate among Keynesian, monetarist, and supply-side viewpoints is not over as each camp will surely wage intellectual battle for supremacy in economic policy-making for the future.

References

Barro, R.J. (2009) Voodoo Multipliers. *Economists' Voice*, 6 (2), 1–4.

Bernanke, B.S. (2000) *Essays on the Great Depression*. Princeton, NJ: Princeton University Press.

Eichenbaum, M. (1997) Some Thoughts on Practical Stabilization Policy. *American Economic Review*, 87 (2), 236–239.

Feldstein, M. (2002) *The Role for Discretionary Fiscal Policy in a Low Interest Rate Environment*. National Bureau of Economic Research Working Paper 9203.

Feldstein, M. (2009) Rethinking the Role of Fiscal Policy. *American Economic Review*, 99 (2), 556–559.

Friedman, M. and Schwartz, A.J. (1963) *A Monetary History of the United States, 1867–1960*. Princeton, NJ: Princeton University Press.

Gwartney, J.D. (2008) Supply-Side Economics. In Henderson, D.R. (Eds.), *The Concise Encyclopedia of Economics* (pp. 482–485). Indianapolis: Liberty Fund.

Henderson, D.R. (Ed.) (2008) *The Concise Encyclopedia of Economics*. Indianapolis: Liberty Fund.

Ip, G. (2005) Long Study of Great Depression Has Shaped Bernanke's Views. *Wall Street Journal*. December 7, 2005.

Keynes, J.M. (1936) *The General Theory of Employment, Interest and Money*. Basingstoke, Hampshire: Palgrave Macmillan.

McCallum, B.T. (2008) Monetarism. In Henderson, D.R. (Eds.), *The Concise Encyclopedia of Economics* (pp. 350–353). Indianapolis: Liberty Fund.

McEachern, W.A. (2007) *Macroeconomics: A Contemporary Introduction*, 7th ed. Mason, OH: Thomson South-Western.

Weil, D.N. (2008) Fiscal Policy. In Henderson, D.R. (Eds.), *The Concise Encyclopedia of Economics* (pp. 182–185). Indianapolis: Liberty Fund.

3

FREE TRADE
Helping Ourselves While Helping Others

Dwight R. Lee

How many people in America (or any other wealthy country) would answer "yes" to the question: Would you favor a government policy that reduced your prosperity, and that of your children, to make it more difficult for poor people in poor countries to escape poverty? Surely this is a silly question. Only someone having a very bad day would answer "yes" to this question. Of course, as everyone knows, the answer you get to a question depends on how it is worded. So consider the following question: Do you favor government restrictions on trade with foreign countries paying very low wages to protect the high-wage jobs of American workers? Though the wording is different, the two questions are really the same, as is explained in this chapter. Yet, a large percentage of the American public, often a majority, answer the latter question in the affirmative. The public opposition in America to international trade was reflected during the 2008 presidential campaign in calls from prominent politicians for a "time out" in negotiating new agreements to expand international trade, with some promising to reduce that trade by canceling existing trade agreements (CNN, 2008).

The point is not that large numbers of Americans are so callous that they would sacrifice some of their own prosperity to keep people in underdeveloped countries impoverished. They wouldn't, at least not intentionally. Instead, the point is that there is a widespread misunderstanding regarding the effects of free trade, with many people sincerely believing that without import restrictions high-paid American workers could not compete against low-paid foreign workers, and would either have to accept much lower pay or be relegated to permanent unemployment. Given this misunderstanding, the resistance to free trade is best explained, not by any hostility by Americans to poor foreigners improving their lives, but by the aversion we all have to becoming worse off.

Since the end of World War II, the United States championed increasing international trade. The lessons of the 1930s were very much on the minds of policy leaders after the war. The Smoot-Hawley Tariff Act of 1930 raised tariffs on 20,000 imported goods. U.S. trade partners in Europe and Canada swiftly retaliated. Businesses lost international customers. Consumers lost access to less expensive goods and services. The standards of living were reduced among all of the trade partners, in the midst of the largest economic downturn in history.

What about more recent events? The U.S. economy took an historic nose-dive in 2007–2010. It was the worst downturn since the Great Depression. Gross Domestic Product (GDP) declined in five out of six quarters from 2008 to the first half of 2009. At the start of the recession in December 2007, the number of unemployed people was 7.5 million, and the unemployment rate was 4.9 percent. The unemployment rate hit a high of 10.1 percent in October 2009. The number of unemployed people increased to 15.7 million. In February 2010, the unemployment rate was 9.7 percent. The number of unemployed people was 14.9 million. This is a far cry from the 25 percent unemployment rate of 1933, but this generation has never seen anything like it.

Should American citizens yearn for a return to the days of Smoot-Hawley? Let's hope not. In the next section I will use the fundamental concepts of scarcity, opportunity cost, and comparative advantage to explain why international trade increases American incomes and is the most effective way we could help poor people in poor countries increase their incomes as well. Favoring trade restrictions really is the same as favoring making both ourselves and poor people in foreign countries worse off.

The Economic Case for Free Trade

Two Implications of Scarcity
The fear that high-paid American workers cannot compete against low-paid foreign workers without import restrictions may seem

plausible, but it vaporizes when confronted with straightforward economic analysis. American workers do receive far higher salaries and wages than most foreign workers, but that does not mean that American workers cost more. High-paid American workers cost less than low-paid foreign workers in the production of many goods and services. The economic case for freer trade is that it increases the pay of American workers by shifting them into jobs where they are less costly than foreign workers. This statement will sound surprising to non-economists, but it follows directly from the implications of *scarcity*—the basis of all economic analysis, and a fact of life with which everyone is familiar.

Scarcity follows directly from our limited ability to produce desirable things and our unlimited ability to want more of them. Two implications of scarcity are directly relevant to the benefits derived from international trade. The first is *opportunity cost*. Scarcity means that doing more of one thing always requires doing less of something else. The opportunity cost of everything we do is the value we sacrifice by having less time and resources to do other things. This cost may, but doesn't always, involve spending money. The cost of spending money on something is the value we could have received by doing something else with the money. On the other hand, we can take a walk along a beach and admire the sunset without spending a dime, but the cost is the value we could otherwise have realized by spending the time doing something else, like visiting a sick friend. The concept of opportunity cost is obvious once stated. But the logical consequences of opportunity costs are commonly ignored when people discuss international trade.

A second implication of scarcity is that we should take advantage of opportunities to produce things with fewer workers. Doing so pushes back the limits of scarcity by allowing more of the things we value to be produced with the same number of workers. This is also obvious, yet many people resist technological progress by arguing that it eliminates jobs. And it does. For example, technological progress eliminated jobs manufacturing electric typewriters. But it created more productive jobs making personal computers and word-processing software, which provided consumers with more value than did typewriters. Over 40 percent of our labor force was required to produce our food in 1900. Technological progress has eliminated most of those jobs, and today about 3 percent of American workers are producing *more food per capita* than over 40 percent did earlier (Federal Reserve Bank of Dallas, 2007; Lebergott, 2002). But the tens of millions of workers released from farm work didn't become permanently unemployed. Instead they moved into other jobs and today some of them, and their descendants, are working in safer and higher-paying jobs producing a host of wonderful goods and services that we have now only because technological progress eliminated those agricultural jobs.

Opportunity Cost and Comparative Advantage

International trade has the same effect as technological progress. International trade makes it possible for workers in all countries to produce more goods, and earn higher wages, by specializing in those jobs where they are most productive, and exchanging some portion of their output for goods produced more productively in other countries. As we are about to see, workers are most productive in those jobs where their opportunity cost is the lowest. This leads to the surprising result that even if workers in a country are better at producing all goods than workers in every other country, they still benefit from international trade.

This result is easily illustrated with an example of two countries, America and China, and two goods, computers and cars. Keeping the discussion as simple as possible, I assume the number of workers required to produce a given output is the only difference in production costs. To highlight the power of international trade, I assume American workers are better than Chinese workers at producing both goods—the same number of workers produces more of both computers and cars in America than in China.

One might conclude that in this situation America has nothing to gain by trading with China. This conclusion is wrong, as is easily shown by considering Table 3.1. The table shows that 100 workers can produce 1,000 computers per week in America, but only 500 per week in China. The table also shows that 100 workers can produce 100 cars per week in America, but only 25 cars per week in China.

Table 3.1 Weekly Output of 100 Workers

	COMPUTERS	CARS
America	1,000	100
China	500	25

Obviously America is better in an absolute sense at producing both computers and cars—it has what economists refer to as an *absolute advantage* over China at producing both goods. But this doesn't mean America can produce both goods at less cost than can China. Indeed, China can produce computers at less cost than America can. As seen from the table, producing 1,000 computers in China requires a sacrifice—opportunity cost—of only 50 cars, while the opportunity cost of producing the same 1,000 computers in America is 100 cars. Economists refer to this as China having a *comparative advantage* in computer production—the productivity at producing computers *compared* to the productivity at producing cars is greater in China than it is in America. On the other hand, producing 100 cars in America would cost only 1,000 computers compared to the 2,000 computers it would cost to produce the same 100 cars in China. America has the comparative advantage in car production.

Both America and China can do better specializing in producing the product in which it has a comparative advantage and trading with the other country for the other product, than by producing both products domestically. For example, if America offers China cars at the "price" of 1,500 computers for 100 cars, America would get 1,500 computers by giving up 100 cars, instead of getting only 1,000 computers for 100 cars without trade. And China would benefit from accepting the offer since it could then get 100 cars for 1,500 computers instead of getting only 75 cars for 1,500 computers without trade.

Notice that both countries can be seen to benefit from trade without any mention of how much workers are being paid. American workers are cheaper in the production of cars than Chinese workers in terms of computers sacrificed per car produced. And this is true regardless of how much American and Chinese workers are paid. Similarly, Chinese workers are cheaper in the production of computers than American workers in terms of cars sacrificed—again, regardless of pay in the two countries. This doesn't mean that the amount workers are paid is unimportant. With free trade, wages provide information on how productive workers are in different jobs, and motivate workers to seek employment where their productivity is highest because that is where wages are highest. Pay will be higher in America than China because American workers have an absolute advantage in producing both products over Chinese workers. But workers in each country receive higher pay when their wages are determined by international competition, because those wages direct workers into the jobs where they have a comparative advantage in productivity, which is the same as where they have the lowest opportunity cost.

We can use our example to consider a complaint about international trade that most of us have heard. It is common when import restrictions are reduced in a country for producers in that country who start losing sales to a foreign country (like American computer producers losing sales to China in our example) to make the following complaint: Since we are more productive at making computers in America than the Chinese are, the only way China can be outcompeting us in computer production is by "dumping" computers in America—selling them below their cost of production. One cannot rule out governments doing silly things, but subsidizing domestic producers to sell their products for less than it cost to make them is a path to poverty, not prosperity. A more likely explanation, as illustrated in our example, is that Chinese computer producers are *not* outcompeting American computer producers. Instead, American car companies are outcompeting American computer companies for labor and other inputs because those resources are more productive manufacturing cars than computers in America. American computer manufacturers cannot match the wages American car manufacturers are willing to pay for workers and compete successfully against Chinese computer manufacturers.

So despite widespread fears, imports don't reduce employment opportunities in a country. Rather, they eliminate some jobs by creating more productive ones. When a country's comparative advantages change in response to changing economic conditions, wages and prices also change in ways that direct workers and resources out of jobs where they have become relatively less valuable and into those where they have become relatively more valuable. These changes don't happen instantly, and they typically result in some transitional unemployment. But because there are many goods in the real world, as opposed to our simple example, these shifts in employment, though taking place constantly, seldom affect more than a small percentage of the work force at any time. While some workers experience temporary unemployment as they make the transition into new, and more productive, jobs, the increased productivity that results increases the general level of real salaries and wages.

True, not everyone who loses his job because of international trade gets a new one that pays better. But even those who earn less in their new jobs are generally earning more than they would if they remained in their old jobs after economic conditions change. For example, after personal computers and word-processing software became available (whether through trade or domestic production), workers who lost their jobs making electric typewriters surely earned more in their new jobs than they could have making typewriters that very few people wanted. Furthermore, every dollar a worker earns in new jobs buys more and better goods because he lives in an economy where other workers also shift into more productive jobs when their old jobs become less productive because of changing conditions. (Even if a country refused to trade with other countries, adjusting to changes in technologies and preferences would still require worker relocation from jobs adding less consumer value to jobs adding more. International trade increases the value of goods and services available to consumers without adding much, if any, to the need for workers to shift between jobs.)

Of course, each worker would like her job and salary protected against both foreign and domestic competition, while she continued to benefit from other workers having to remain responsive to her desires by having to change jobs. But would she favor trade restrictions protecting her job and salary if it meant that everyone else received the same protection? Not likely. Still, as we shall see below, the desire for workers to have just their jobs protected has important implications for the politics of international trade.

The simple economic logic of opportunity cost and comparative advantage makes it clear that Americans would benefit from freer trade.

But it also makes clear that people in smaller, and generally poorer, countries would benefit far more. America is a large free-trade zone that allows us to benefit more from relying entirely on domestic trade than can small countries. There are many small poor countries whose citizens have comparative advantages in only a few products—far fewer than they need for their own consumption. Without import restrictions in wealthy countries, these poor countries could benefit enormously, while benefiting those in the wealthy countries, by specializing in producing the few goods in which they have a comparative advantage and trading them to other countries in return for the many other goods that can be imported more cheaply than produced domestically. The most effective way wealthy countries can help poor people in other countries escape poverty, while simultaneously increasing their own prosperity, would be by reducing restrictions on trading with them. By doing so those of us in wealthy countries would benefit from the comparative advantages of those in poor countries while letting them benefit from ours.

Some Unanswered Questions

Our simple example of comparative advantage leaves some questions unanswered. I consider two that deserve consideration. First, in our U.S.–China example a country either produced a good or imported it, but not both. Yet in the real world countries both produce and import the same goods—computers and cars for example. Is this consistent with the concept of comparative advantage, which in our example implied that a country should either produce or import a good, but not both? And second, why don't all countries eliminate, or at least greatly reduce, restrictions on international trade if they would benefit from doing so?

The answer to the first question is that the implication that a country should either produce a good or import it is the result of two simplifying assumptions in our example. The first simplifying assumption is that there are only two goods and that each good is the same no matter which country makes it. A computer is the same whether it is made in America or China and so is a car. The second assumption is that the cost of producing another unit of one good in terms of the sacrifice of the other good is always the same within a country. No matter how many cars are produced in America, the average and marginal cost of producing cars in America is ten computers in our example. Similarly, no matter how many computers are produced in China the average and marginal cost of producing computers in China is 1/20th of a car.

In the more realistic case, where there is more than one type of car, America could have a comparative advantage in producing some varieties, or brands, of cars and China could have a comparative advantage in producing others. So types of cars that America has a comparative advantage in producing would be produced in America and sold to consumers in both America and China, while some American consumers would import cars from China which it has a comparative advantage in producing. Thus, America would both produce and import cars. Similarly, China could both produce and import cars. And, using the same reasoning, America could have a comparative advantage producing one type of computer and China a comparative advantage in producing another type, with each country both producing and importing computers.

But even if all cars and all computers are identical, whether made in America or China, the principle of comparative advantage can still call for a country to both produce and import the same good once we drop the assumption that marginal production costs are constant. For example, when both countries are producing no cars, America may be able to produce them at a lower marginal cost in terms of forgone computers than China, which means that China will initially be able to produce computers at a lower marginal cost in terms of forgone cars than America. But as America produces more cars and no computers, and China produces more computers and no cars, it can happen that increasing marginal production costs of producing cars in America and computers in China eventually results in the comparative advantage switching, at the margin. At this point America will be able to produce additional computers cheaper than China and China will be able to produce additional cars cheaper than America, at least for a while. The ideal production mix would be for both countries to produce computers and cars in amounts that equalize the marginal production cost of each good in both countries. (Equalizing the marginal production cost of computers in terms of forgone cars in America and China necessarily equalizes the marginal production costs of cars in term of forgone computers in each country.) This production mix is highly unlikely to find each country producing the mix of computers and cars that consumers in each country want to consume. Instead, one country will likely end up both producing and importing one of the goods, and the other country both producing and importing the other good.

But if all countries would benefit from eliminating most, if not all, trade restrictions, why haven't more countries done so? The answer follows from the observation of "public choice" economists (those who apply economic analysis to study the political process) that political decisions are more responsive to small but narrowly focused benefits than to larger but widely diffused costs. An import restriction typically concentrates benefits on the relatively few who are invested in, and working for, the industry being protected against foreign competition. Furthermore, these investors and workers are typically organized around their interest in the profitability of the protected industry, which makes it easier for them to exercise political influence. Although the costs of the import restriction are greater than the benefits, those costs are dispersed over many consumers who buy a multitude of different goods and therefore are not likely to be affected much by a higher price on one of those goods.

As this chapter was being written, President Obama announced that he was going to impose a 35 percent tariff on imported tires for cars and light trucks from China (Weisman, 2009). The cost of this tariff to American consumers will exceed the benefit to the relatively few American workers making tires. But the union representing the tire workers was far more active and effective politically in their support of the tariff than unorganized consumers were in opposing it. In the case of international trade, as in other cases, politicians often find that their desire to increase campaign contributions and get re-elected trumps their desire to serve the public interest.

Conclusion

The primary purpose of this chapter has been to explain the strictly economic advantages from free international trade. Freer trade would increase our wealth and the wealth of those with whom we trade. But the economic gains from international trade are a byproduct of benefits that many consider more important. The economic advantages of international trade are the direct result of its ability to promote harmonious and productive relationships between countless people from diverse cultural backgrounds and ethnic origins—exactly the type of cultural diversity for which so many contemporary critics of international trade express enthusiasm. International trade encourages people from all over the world, with various languages, religious beliefs, interests, and skills to profit from their differences by specializing their efforts in ways that best serve their mutual interests. Free trade penalizes parochialism and cultural isolation and rewards those who expand their markets by expanding their knowledge of, and increasing their sensitivity to, those with a wide variety of culturally influenced interests and concerns.

No sensible person would argue that freer trade would solve all of our economic problems and eliminate all international conflict. But it would be equally foolish for those sincerely interested in reducing poverty and international conflict to ignore the ability of freer trade to help promote global prosperity and harmony.

References

CNN. (2008, February 21). The CNN Democratic presidential debate in Texas. Retrieved from: www.cnn.com/2008/POLITICS/02/21/debate. transcript.

Federal Reserve Bank of Dallas. (2007). *Annual report: Opportunity knocks—selling our services to the world.* Retrieved from: www.dallasfed.org/fed/annual/2007/ar07.pdf.

Lebergott, S. (2002). Wages and working conditions. In *The Concise encyclopedia of economics.* Retrieved from: www.econlib.org/library/Enc1/WagesandWorkingConditions.html.

Weisman, J. (2009, September 13). U.S. to impose tariff on Chinese tires. *Wall Street Journal,* Retrieved from: http://online.wsj.com/article/SB1252718242 37605479.html.

4

Public Choice and Behavioral Economics

Implications for Instructors in an Uncertain Economic Environment

Angela M. Smith and
William C. Wood

In a fast-food restaurant with four service counters, would you expect to see a big difference in the number of people in line at the counters, as illustrated below?

No; ordinarily we would expect some of the people in the longest line to move. This might continue until all four lines were approximately equal in length. When all customers were content to stay in their existing lines, they would be in "equilibrium," as economics uses the concept. As consumers sought the shortest lines we would consider their behavior purposeful or "rational."

What does this example have to do with the economic turmoil of 2008–2009 and beyond? As we will see, the answer to this question lies in the concept of rational equilibrium. Rational equilibrium is a powerful concept in economics, but it does not lend itself to exact conclusions. If we concluded "the length of fast-food service lines will always be equalized," we would not be correct. We would be

attributing too much rationality and precision to an equilibrium model, when we know that misperceptions, mistakes, and balky cash registers can get in the way of equalizing lines.

If we say fast-food service lines will always equalize, we make the mistake of putting *too much* trust in a rational equilibrium model. But to say "we cannot predict anything about service lines" makes the opposite mistake, that of putting *too little* trust in a rational equilibrium model. There are significant behavior patterns at work, and we cannot learn much if we ignore them.

When we expand the subject from fast-food service lines to the economic structural changes of 2008–2009 and beyond, it becomes even more important to put the right degree of trust in equilibrium models. Social studies instructors whose teaching reflects too much or too little trust may not be fully equipping students with the tools needed to understand some types of observed behavior. The distinctive fields of public choice and behavioral economics show why.

Those whose teaching reflects a government that always operates in the public interest may put too little trust in the rational model, failing to account for the impact of self-interested behavior by government officials on some public policy outcomes. These instructors could gain from the insights of public choice, which addresses these issues by bringing many aspects of the rational model into the study of public decision-making.

On the other hand, those whose teaching reflects a belief that consumers always operate rationally may put too much trust in the rational model, failing to account for various limits on individual rationality and other emotional and psychological responses that affect some decisions. These instructors could benefit from more understanding of behavioral economics, which relaxes the rigidity of the rational model. It incorporates a broader variety of behaviors that do not easily fit into the optimizing framework in order to better understand and predict individual choices.

This chapter provides an introduction to the two related fields, with teaching suggestions and activities for each. We believe our exploration of public choice and behavioral economics can help instructors discover implicit assumptions behind their teaching that may need revision in light of some events relating to the 2008–2009 crisis such as the housing bubble and sub-prime mortgage crisis, the behavior of Fannie Mae and Freddie Mac, the government bailouts of financial and automotive firms, and the decline in various asset markets.

Public Choice

Most of us learned in a history class that the early twentieth century was a time of "robber barons" who had to be reined in by a government seeking the public interest. We may not have heard that some of the "robber barons" themselves sought to be regulated. Why would these powerful executives voluntarily seek limitations on their own freedoms and why would their desires be granted by politicians? Answering such questions requires abandoning a single-minded view that governments always seek the public interest and adopting instead a richer view that accounts for the self-interests of executives and government officials alike.

Traditionally, economic instruction largely neglected such possibilities. A survey of economics textbooks used in high school courses (Leet and Lopus, 2007), for example, showed that most textbooks do not even cover the National Voluntary Content Standard 17 about government failure (National Council on Economic Education, 2009). The standard, labeled "Using Cost/Benefit Analysis to Evaluate Government Programs," says:

> Costs of government policies sometimes exceed benefits. This may occur because of incentives facing voters, government officials, and government employees, because of actions by special interest groups that can impose costs on the general public, or because social goals other than economic efficiency are being pursued.

This standard, placed in counterpoint to Standard 16 about market failure, makes it clear that our economy can have neither perfect markets nor perfect governments in all situations. It provides the background for teaching students about the appropriate mix of markets and government to meet economic policy challenges.

Incorporating this richer view of behavior—that both private citizens and public officials rationally respond to incentives by promoting their own interests—lies at the heart of public choice. The public choice view allows for market success and government success, for market failure and government failure. It also provides opportunities for classroom teaching to explain how governments work in far more realistic terms. Applying the rational model to politics generates a number of important findings, including that:

- firms might choose to actively seek out regulations and the political system may grant these regulations, regardless of whether they benefit a majority of citizens or consumers;
- government bureaucracies motivated by self-interest might not act to maximize efficiency or the public welfare;
- ordinary voting can be vulnerable to strategic manipulation; and
- there can exist both a lack of participation and ignorance even among some rational citizen voters.

There are two main factors, both central to public choice, that drive most of the conclusions stated above. First, the government is not some entity purely motivated by a benevolent desire to benefit society but instead it is a collection of individuals who are assumed to serve primarily their own private self-interests. These interests may be to get elected (or re-elected) or to achieve a higher degree of power, status, or money. That is not to say there are no government officials that care about truly seeking the public benefit, but only that individual self-interests are not ignored and indeed play an important role in decision-making even in the public realm. The second factor is that voting, both by citizens and politicians, is the primary method of preference aggregation in many democracies. The nature of voting has important implications for behavior, including a lack of voter participation and knowledge as well as logrolling and vote trading among politicians.

Assuming that government officials are motivated by the self-interest of getting elected (or re-elected) can help lead us to many of the important findings in public choice. Consider the concept of regulation. It is easy to understand why profit-motivated industries might seek out regulation such as import quotas, tariffs, or other policies, when that regulation limits competition or entry of new firms.

What is more subtle is that self-interested politicians have an incentive to acquiesce to the demands for regulation from some industries (Stigler, 1971; Peltzman, 1976; Beard et al., 2007). A candidate that earns favor from special interests by supporting their desired policies is likely to benefit in the form of many votes for election and potentially large campaign contributions. If the politician is primarily interested in getting elected, these benefits go a long way toward that goal. This increase in election probability from supporting the policies often outweighs any negative response by citizen voters since the costs imposed on any one individual voter are small and citizens may not be fully informed to begin with (see below). Thus, a government official might have the incentive to support regulation pushed by these industries or policies desired by mobilized special interest groups even if these policies make many citizens worse off.

The self-interested motivation of government officials can also help explain the lack of efficient use of resources by government agencies and bureaucracies. Think of a government agency as producing a "good" such as regulation or education. Those who work in the agency are likely to be motivated by their own interests, which might include salary, power, reputation, and office perks. Many of these interests tend to be correlated with the size of the bureau and, more specifically, with the size of the budget received by the bureau from the government. In this case, bureaucracies may have the incentive to try to make their budgets as large as possible, and not to undertake cost-cutting (Niskanen, 1971; Blais and Dion, 2004).

The nature of voting also has important implications for public choice. First, let us consider voting by citizens in elections. Since one vote is very unlikely to have any effect on the outcome of most elections, many individuals may rationally decide not to vote. They would reason that the costs of voting, however small, outweigh the benefit that is expected to only be received with a minute probability. Indeed, voter participation in elections is significantly less than 100 percent in the United States; it tends to be below 60 percent in general for presidential elections and even smaller for state and local elections. Another aspect of citizen voting is that many individuals may find it too costly in terms of time and effort to learn various details about voting history and stated positions of all potential candidates. If they are unlikely to affect the outcome, individual voters (even rational ones) may find themselves somewhat ignorant about the issues and the candidates. They are ignorant, but "rationally ignorant" (Downs, 1957).

When the politicians of a board or assembly vote, in contrast to millions of citizens voting, the significantly smaller numbers have important implications. In some situations, the outcome of a vote depends on the order in which different issues are considered or the agenda, leaving the agenda-maker with potential power to affect the outcome (Plott and Levine, 1978; Bernheim et al., 2006). Also, since there are a number of votes taken on various issues with the same elected officials, there might be an incentive for representatives to "trade" votes, which is also known as logrolling. Representatives may find it beneficial to vote for a policy they weakly oppose if, by doing so, another colleague will promise to vote for a policy they strongly favor (Tullock and Buchanan, 1962; Stratmann, 1992). Increasing the likelihood with which their strongly favored proposal (or one that is strongly favored by their constituents) passes might overpower any negative response from voting for a weakly opposed policy.

The main concepts brought to light by public choice are important to consider in general but also relevant to recent economic events through the crisis of 2008–2009. One example can be found pre-meltdown in the governmental push to expand homeownership and make it available to everyone including minorities and lower-income groups. To accommodate these goals, the government subsidized and encouraged homeownership through a number of policies including relaxation of credit standards and underwriting criteria guidelines as well as tax benefits for homeowners.

These programs were likely popular at the time of conception both in the eyes of want-to-be-homeowners as well as special interest groups, thus providing one possible motive (i.e., votes) for government officials to support the initiatives. This popular support is at least suggested by the rise in the homeownership rate following implementation of these policies (U.S. Census, 2008) combined with the stated interests of groups such as the National Association of Realtors (2009), which "seeks to be the leading advocate of the right to own, use, and transfer real property" and the National Association of Home Builders (2009), which "helps promote the policies that make housing a national priority." However, these same programs are now blamed in part for the sub-prime mortgage crisis in which many risky loans granted under the looser credit standards went into default and homeowners were forced into foreclosure (Gwartney et al., 2009).

Another application of public choice relates to the structure of governmental policies surrounding the financial institutions of Fannie Mae and Freddie Mac that were designed to facilitate housing finance. Fannie Mae and Freddie Mac are government-sponsored enterprises (GSEs), which means that they are privately owned corporations that also have the backing of the U.S. government. Thus, these firms have shareholders that control decision-making and earn profits based on the company's success but they also receive certain benefits as well as a credit line to the U.S. Treasury due to the governmental support.

While Fannie Mae and Freddie Mac have experienced a great deal of growth in past years, the recent crisis highlights some of the underlying incentives of this type of government-sponsored firm. For example, they might have an incentive to take on a more than optimal level of risk since the benefits accrue privately to the owners while any costly failures are primarily borne by the government and thus spread out across numerous taxpayers. This "heads, I win; tails, you lose" incentive structure might have played a part in sub-prime lending and other practices. The privatization of gains and socialization of losses described for these entities also helps to explain the continued existence of policies that support them. This is true because the special interests of groups are more likely to be represented in policies when the benefits are concentrated among relatively few individuals while the costs are spread out thinly against numerous unorganized citizens (Olson, 1971).

In addition to the events leading up to the financial crisis, there were numerous policies enacted in the initial aftermath, including several large bailouts by the federal government of both financial institutions and automotive manufacturers. These bailouts were prompted primarily by concerns of both lost jobs and further economic chaos from firm failure. The financially supported firms cer-

a test. Stock investors may overestimate their ability to pick winners and avoid losers in the market. Research suggests that overconfidence by some investors can also lead to excessive trading, which lowers expected benefits (Barber and Odean, 2001). Also, a survey found that over 80 percent of people believe that they are above-average drivers (Svenson, 1981). This clear overconfidence on the part of some drivers may encourage them to be less careful while driving than what is optimal given their true ability.

Another pattern of human behavior is to overweight recent information even when past events are relevant either because individuals have limited memory or just selective memory that focuses on the latest data. This behavioral response has been noted in experiments where individuals acting as firms underweight past demand for products in favor of more recent observations of demand (Bostian et al., 2008). Also, this recency effect may be present when individuals are determining the underlying value of their house or another asset such as a stock. Even in experimental markets, asset price "bubbles" are prevalent where asset prices increase (and then crash) without a fundamental explanation (Smith et al., 1988). These bubbles could potentially be explained by many behavioral factors including overweighting of recent information and overconfidence.

While the rational model often assumes accurate incorporation of risk or the probability of an event into expected payoffs, behavioral economics has found that individuals tend to misperceive risk in various situations. Often, this manifests itself in the overweighting of small-probability events and underweighting of high-probability events or in the inaccurate incorporation of new information into prior probabilities (Tversky and Kahneman, 1992). Someone getting ready to take an air trip may overestimate the chances of crashing if there has been a recent air crash in the news. Hammerton (1973) found a similar behavioral tendency when he studied subjects' processing of detailed information about the likelihood of a disease. Even with information about the population and the likelihood of a false positive, subjects still tended to overestimate the probability of actually having the disease given a positive test result.

Lastly, in cases where calculating or comparing the costs and benefits of actions is difficult, time-consuming, or costly, some individuals may exhibit what is known as "bounded rationality" (Simon, 1957; Kahneman, 2003). Those who exhibit bounded rationality may make mistakes by failing to choose optimal decisions. In these situations, individuals stray from cost–benefit analysis and may resort to customs or rules of thumb that help govern their behavior. Their behavior is "rational" in the sense that, given their calculations or rules, they make predictable patterned decisions that are not random. However, since choices fail to maximize their benefit given the cost, the rationality is not perfect but "bounded" instead. For example, faced with three estimates for building a fence, consumers might have a tendency to choose the middle estimate to avoid both overpayment and sloppy workmanship. The individual might continue to make this choice even in the midst of neighbor comments vouching for the more expensive fence company. However, with more time and reflection, the individual might have made a more optimal choice.

These behavioral departures from strict rationality have important implications for the current economy and help us to understand some aspects of the 2008–2009 crisis. Alan Greenspan, Chairman of the Federal Reserve from 1987 to 2006, felt in hindsight that he had initially put too much trust in the rational optimizing model as he failed to predict the latest economic meltdown. In testimony before the House Committee on Oversight and Government Reform (2008), he stated: "Those of us who have looked to the self-interest of lending institutions to protect shareholders' equity (myself especially), are in a state of shocked disbelief." Not only are organizations, made up of individuals with behavioral tendencies, potentially fallible but consumers are as well. Greenspan points this out in an article in the *Financial Times* (2008) as he mentions the need for forecasters to incorporate observable and systematic behavioral responses, even if they are labeled "non-rational."

Specific examples of the pertinent themes of behavioral economics can be found scattered throughout recent economic events. For instance, the housing bubble that subsequently crashed was propped up in part by risky sub-prime mortgage loans that consumers purchased. While these mortgages may have been offered by financial institutions due to relaxed credit standards and other policies, a number of behavioral tendencies are likely involved in a consumer's decision to actually purchase a home with a risky mortgage. First, consumers may have been overconfident that they would be able to afford the mortgage payments and that housing prices would continue to rise bringing them profits as opposed to foreclosure notices. Also, the tendency to focus on recent events may have both boosted the perception that housing prices would continue to rise and made adjustable-rate mortgages seem more attractive and less risky to consumers since interest rates had been relatively low in recent history. The total adjustable-rate mortgage amounts (both conventional and government) skyrocketed from $622,698 million in 2000 to $2,272,432 million in 2004 (Federal Housing Finance Agency, 2009). Moreover, if consumers are unable to accurately perceive risk, they may be more inclined to make sub-optimal decisions regarding the affordability and risk level involved in the purchase of a particular home. Lastly, the purchase of a home and selection of a mortgage instrument is an extremely complex decision. Bounded rationality may inhibit some consumers from fully processing all relevant information and leave them to rely on educated guesses, experience-based methods, or on the advice of others such as the mortgage-granting financial institution. For example, an individual that is approved for a loan up to $417,000 by the bank may use that as a measure of how much he or she can afford to pay for a house. This may prove not to be optimal once present and future individual-specific financial situations and goals are taken into account.

The collapse of the housing market was an important catalyst of the crisis but financial panic continued in the aftermath. Some behavior in the midst of this panic can also be linked to or possibly explained by patterns highlighted in behavioral economics. For example, once the crisis began, recency effects combined with other factors may have altered individual and firm perceptions causing them to project markets to fall further. It is possible that this caused individuals to sell their assets at a sub-optimal time. Also, if there was misperception of elevated risks such as unemployment, individuals might be led to make savings and consumption decisions that are not individually optimal and have important ramifications for the economy as a whole. These selected examples demonstrate that the themes of behavioral economics have important implications both for everyday consumer behavior and for the economy as a whole.

As with public choice, classroom activities designed to illustrate concepts can be useful when discussing behavioral economics. One short activity may ask students: "Relative to your classmates, are you an average driver, above average, or below average?" After collecting responses, it is likely that well over half of the students feel that they fall in the above-average category. This can be used to introduce the idea of overconfidence. There are other classroom games illustrating behavioral economics concepts including those relevant to asset price bubbles (Ball and Holt, 1998) and Bayes' rule calculations (Holt and Anderson, 1996).

Conclusion

Public choice and behavioral economics help us see the world more realistically. Through careful application of rational models in some areas, and thoughtful extensions in other areas, scholars have deepened our understanding of human behavior in markets and in governments. These disciplines offer insight as one explores both the motivation for policies and the resulting outcomes.

Proposed consumer finance protections offer a concluding example. In the wake of 2008–2009's economic stresses, a Consumer Finance Protection Agency was proposed to protect consumers from making mistakes in borrowing and lending. As the legislative process continued, it was unclear whether the new protections would be concentrated in a single new agency or allocated across existing agencies. In either case, the concept likely arose because mistakes in sub-prime mortgage markets compounded by bad policy were blamed for the financial market meltdown.

Traditional ways of understanding and teaching regulation would be inadequate to understanding the proposed regulations' consumer protection mission. The traditional model called "consumer sovereignty" would say that the consumer is king, and any fully informed consumer should not be discouraged from taking out a risky loan or running up a credit card balance. However, behavioral economics informs us that consumers sometimes fail to operate within the traditional rational

Table 4.1 Focus: Understanding Economics in Civics and Government—Selected Lessons

HOW DO CONSTITUTIONS SHAPE ECONOMIC SYSTEMS?

Students examine the characteristics of a market economy and the economic provisions of the U.S. Constitution, as well as explore why two nations, who have so much in common including location, access to natural resources, culture, and language, have very different economic outcomes? Students examine excerpts from the Constitutions of North Korea and South Korea and examine their differences.

"FREE TO DO WHAT I WANT?"

What is the relationship between economic freedom and political freedom? Students brainstorm examples of political and economic freedom, then examine the relationship between two indices: the Freedom House Freedom in the World survey and the Wall Street Journal/Heritage Foundation Index of Economic Freedom. Students analyze and plot data from 30 randomly selected countries to determine if a relationship between the two types of freedom exists.

VOTERS AND ELECTIONS

Students participate in a median voter demonstration and explore "moderate" economic positions between two extreme political views. Students also examine the costs and benefits of voting to figure out why people choose to vote.

WHAT ARE THE ECONOMIC FUNCTIONS OF GOVERNMENT?

The teacher presents six economic functions of government in a brief lecture, and students classify newspaper headlines according to the six functions. A brief reading introduces "liberal" and "conservative" views of the scope of government economic activity. Students work in groups to develop liberal and conservative arguments on one of the newspaper headlines.

GOVERNMENT SPENDING

Students identify patterns and trends in spending by government at the federal, state, and local levels, and analyze the potential problems posed by the growth in federal mandatory spending.

CAN ELECTION FUTURES MARKETS BE MORE ACCURATE THAN POLLS?

Students examine the results of public opinion polls conducted near the end of the 2004 presidential election. They compare the results of several national polls to those of the Iowa Electronic Markets (IEM), a system that used futures markets to predict the outcome of the 2004 race. Students read and discuss a handout which allows a comparison between public opinion polls and the Iowa Electronic Markets.

TAXES CHANGE BEHAVIOR

Students review the economic functions of government and they recognize that taxes are necessary to pay for government activities. Students are shown an example of how a tax on cigarettes raises the price of cigarettes, which decreases smoking, and evaluate how various taxes change the behavior of those to whom they apply. They learn that taxes provide incentives that may have unexpected results.

ECONOMIC MISERY AND THE PRESIDENCY

Students examine economic data in order to predict the results of presidential elections.

The Market Goes to Court: Key Economic Cases and the United States Supreme Court

Students participate in a short "reader's theater" that reviews key roles of the Supreme Court, and introduces students to four types of economic cases heard by the Court. Students then complete a data chart summarizing the four types of economic cases. This lesson can serve as an excellent review/extension activity during a unit on the U.S. Supreme Court.

AN ECONOMIC ANALYSIS OF HEALTH CARE POLICY

Students briefly discuss the strengths and weaknesses of health care in the United States. As "members" of the Surgeon General's Task Force on the Economics of Health Care Policies, the students examine how the laws of supply and demand can be applied to health care. They study four criteria for judging health care policies and then apply those criteria to three general plans: Pay or Play, Tax Credits, and National Health Insurance.

HOW SHOULD GOVERNMENTS STRUCTURE THE TAX SYSTEM?

Students decide on a method of taxation and discuss their reasoning for designing the type of tax system they have created. They learn whether their system is progressive, regressive, or proportional.

model, causing them to make sub-optimal decisions. That knowledge could potentially underlie the stated consumer protection goal.

On the other hand, the traditional model might lend support to the need for new consumer finance protection as a benevolent attempt to rein in the overwhelming power of financial institutions in the name of the greater good. However, lessons from public choice remind us that many policies are motivated not by an overwhelming desire to serve the public and consumers but by the self-interests of the government officials involved in the decision. Thus, one becomes cautious about the ability of the proposed policies to regulate in the public's interest and is prone to seek out more detailed information regarding the anticipated effects of the policy.

Although traditional curricula have largely ignored the findings of public choice and behavioral economics, newer materials are correcting the deficiency. A new publication from the Council for Economic Education, *Focus: Understanding Economics in Civics and Government* (2010) provides an example. Selected lessons are outlined in Table 4.1. The lesson on "Voters and Elections" shows some strategic implications of voting and also explores the benefits and costs of voting to help students understand who votes. Lessons such as this can give students a far deeper analytical understanding of voting behavior than is possible without the insights of public choice. In a similar way, the lesson entitled "Taxes Change Behavior" can help students toward a full understanding of taxes not just as neutral revenue raisers, but as instruments of policy that change behavior.

With greater knowledge of the insights of public choice and behavioral economics, instructors can promote a balanced understanding among their students. Instruction is far more useful if it acknowledges the existence of imperfect markets, imperfect governments and boundedly rational consumers.

References

Ball, S.B. and Holt, C.A. (1998). Classroom games: Bubbles in an asset market. *Journal of Economic Perspectives*, 12(1), 207–218.

Barber, B. and Odean, T. (2001). Boys will be boys: Gender, overconfidence, and common stock investment. *Quarterly Journal of Economics*, 116, 261–292.

Beard, T.R., Kaserman, D.L., and Mayo, J.W. (2007). A graphical approach to the Stiglerian "theory of regulation." *Journal of Economic Education*, 38(4), 447–451.

Bernheim, B.D., Rangel, A., and Rayo, L. (2006). The power of the last word in legislative policy making. *Econometrica*, 74(5), 1161–1190.

Blais, A. and Dion, S. (2004). Are bureaucrats budget maximizers? The Niskanen model and its critics, in Heckelman, J.C., ed., *Readings in public choice*. Ann Arbor: University of Michigan Press.

Bostian, A.J.A., Holt, C.A., and Smith, A.M. (2008). The Newsvendor pull-to-center effect: Adaptive learning in a laboratory experiment. *Manufacturing and Service Operations Management*, 10(4), 590–608.

Council for Economic Education. (2010). *Focus: Understanding economics in civics and government*. New York: Council for Economic Education.

Delemeester, G. and Brauer, J. (2008). *Games economists play: Non-computerized classroom-games for college economics*. Retrieved from: www.marietta.edu/~delemeeg/games.

Downs, A. (1957). *An Economic theory of democracy*. New York: Harper.

Federal Housing Finance Agency. (2009). *Data on single-family mortgage originations, 1990–2009Q1*. Retrieved from www.fhfa.gov/Default.aspx?Page=70.

Goeree, J.K. and Holt, C.A. (1999). Rent-seeking and the inefficiency of non-market allocation. *Journal of Economic Perspectives*, 13(3), 217–226.

Greenspan, A. (2008). *Testimony in October 2008 to the Committee on Government Oversight and Reform*. March 16, 2008. Retrieved from: http://oversight.house.gov/documents/20081023100438.pdf.

Greenspan, A. (2008). We will never have a perfect model of risk. *Financial Times*. March 16, 2008. Retrieved from: www.ft.com/cms/s/0/edbdbcf6-f360-11dc-b6bc-0000779fd2ac.html?nclick_check=1.

Gwartney, J., Macpherson, D., Sobel, R., and Stroup, R. (2009). *Special topic: Crash of 2008*. Retrieved from: http://commonsenseeconomics.com/Activities/Crisis/CSE.CrashOf2008.pdf.

Hammerton, M. (1973). A case of radical probability estimation. *Journal of Experimental Psychology*, 101, 252–254.

Holt, C.A. (2007). *Markets, games and strategic behavior*. Boston: Pearson Education.

Holt, C.A. (1999). *Y2k bibliography of experimental economics and social science: Classroom games—using experiments in teaching*. Retrieved from: http://people.virginia.edu/~cah2k/classy2k.htm.

Holt, C.A. and Anderson, L.R. (1999). Agendas and strategic voting. *Southern Economic Journal*, 65(3), 622–629.

Holt, C.A. and Anderson, L.R. (1996). Classroom games: Understanding Bayes' rule. *Journal of Economic Perspectives*, 10(2), 179–187.

Kahneman, D. (2003). Maps of bounded rationality: Psychology for behavioral economics. *American Economic Review*, 93(5), 1449–1475.

Leet, D.R. and Lopus, J.S. (2007). Ten observations on high school economics textbooks. *Citizenship, Social and Economics Education: An International Journal*, 7(3), 201–214.

NAHB (National Association of Home Builders). (2009). *About NAHB*. Retrieved from: www.nahb.org/page.aspx/landing/sectionID=5.

NAR (National Association of Realtors). (2009). *NAR's mission and vision*. Retrieved from: www.realtor.org/realtororg.nsf/pages/narmission.

National Council on Economic Education. (1997). *Voluntary national standards in economics*. Retrieved from: www.councilforeconed.org/ea/standards.

Niskanen, W.A. (1971). *Bureaucracy and representative government*. Chicago: Aldine Atherton.

Olson, M. (1971). *The logic of collective action: Public goods and the theory of groups* (rev. ed.). Cambridge, MA: Harvard University Press.

Peltzman, S. (1976). Toward a more general theory of regulation. *Journal of Law and Economics*, 19, 211–240.

Plott, C.R. and Levine, M.E. (1978). A model of agenda influence on committee decisions. *American Economic Review*, 68(1), 146–160.

Simon, H. (1957). A behavioral model of rational choice. In *Models of man, social and rational: Mathematical essays on rational behavior in a social setting*. New York: Wiley.

Smith, V.L., Suchanek, G., and Williams, A. (1988). Bubbles, crashes and endogenous expectations in experimental spot asset markets. *Econometrica*, 56, 1119–1151.

Stigler, G.J. (1971). The theory of economic regulation. *Bell Journal of Economics*, 2(1), 3–21.

Stratmann, T. (1992). The effects of logrolling on congressional voting. *American Economic Review*, 82(5), 1162–1176.

Svenson, O. (1981). Are we all less risky and more skillful than our fellow drivers? *Acta Psychologia*, 47, 143–148.

Tullock, G. and Buchanan, J.M. (1962). *Calculus of consent*. Ann Arbor: University of Michigan Press.

Tversky, A. and Kahneman, D. (1992). Advances in prospect theory: Cumulative representation of uncertainty. *Journal of Risk and Uncertainty*, 5, 297–323.

U.S. Census Bureau. (2009). *Housing vacancies and homeownership*. Retrieved from: www.census.gov/hhes/www/housing/hvs/qtr108/q108tab5.html.

Wight, J.B. and Morton, J.S. (2007). *Teaching the ethical foundations of economics*. New York: National Council on Economic Education.

5

Morality of Markets
Classroom and Conscience

J.R. Clark and Mark C. Schug

One of us recently shared a taxi leaving the meetings of the National Council for the Social Studies and going to the Atlanta airport. We introduced ourselves. She was a historian. He was an economist. After she learned she was sharing a cab with an economist, the mood of the historian immediately darkened. Economics made her uncomfortable, she said. The discipline of economics was somehow tainted in her mind. She is not alone.

This is not the first time economists have encountered this sort of reaction. Many people have difficulty understanding markets because they suspect that markets—and the people who study them—are fundamentally immoral. Don't markets depend on greed? Isn't the private sector corrupt? This chapter will address each of these questions and then explain how markets influence moral behavior.

Morality of Markets for the Classroom: Opportunity Cost and Marginal Analysis

Ethics as a discipline studies values and virtues. Economics as a discipline studies how people make choices. It is not much of a surprise that ethics and economics are intimately connected. We contend that an understanding of the basics of economics may improve our understanding of why people make the moral choices that they do. Helping people sort out what is right and what is wrong is not as easy as some might think. Opinions about what constitutes ethical behavior vary logically from individual to individual and from situation to situation.

We propose that two concepts from economics are very helpful in helping us understand moral decisions—opportunity cost and marginal analysis.

Let's consider the opportunity cost involved in making a moral choice. Consider the case of a child drowning in a swimming pool. Most people would not hesitate to jump into the swimming pool to rescue the drowning child even though the child might be a complete stranger. Conversely, the same people would not be as quick to attempt the rescue if the drowning child had fallen into a raging river. Interestingly enough, parents would be more inclined to jump into the river to save their own child than the child of a stranger.

Why do people respond differently to each drowning situation? After all, a child's life is in danger in each case. The answer lies in recognizing the opportunity costs or the sacrifices involved.

The discipline of economics begins by recognizing the existence of scarcity. Economists rarely tire of pointing out that our wants are unlimited while our productive resources are finite. Even wealthy people face scarcity, if not for any other reason than that time is a resource. We only have so much of it. Scarcity of time means that even the wealthy have to make choices. Bill Gates and Warren Buffet face scarcity. Should they spend time running their businesses? Vacationing in Fiji? Giving away the billions they earned? Scarcity makes economizing, or making choices, unavoidable. Everyone has to do it—saints and sinners alike.

As a result of scarcity, we have to make choices and our choices always involve an opportunity cost. An opportunity cost is the value of the highest valued alternative that must be forgone in making that choice. All choices involve a cost. Always. To some, this unrelenting focus of economists on costs is what makes economics a dismal science. Maybe so. But, it also offers important insights that would be overlooked in a rosier world view.

At high levels of generality, all would agree that life is precious and should be preserved. The discipline of economics reminds us that some sacrifices—even a sacrifice to preserve a life—can be too great because of the costs involved. The choice confronted by the people in the drowning situations is considered in light of the level of sacrifice likely to be made. In the case of the swimming pool rescue, the potential opportunity cost is less. It is highly likely that the rescuer will succeed and both parties will survive. The case of the river rescue is a high-cost choice. If the potential rescuer is a poor swimmer and decided that the river rescue attempt is almost certain to result in two drowned instead of one, few would think it immoral not to dive into the water.

Closely tied to the idea of cost is the concept of marginal analysis. The trade-offs that people make do not have to be all-or-nothing decisions. This is important because additional amounts of almost everything become less valuable to us as we acquire more. Food is an example. We all need food to survive. It is a necessity. This suggests that there is perhaps some moral obligation to provide people some basic level of food and that those who supply food should keep prices at very low levels.

However, the quantity and quality of food people will consume will depend heavily on the price. The good news about "food" in a market economy is that there are all different kinds of it. We don't buy "food" as such. Instead there is this vast array of choices to meet our nutritional desires. Picture yourself walking the aisles of your favorite grocery store. There are dozens of meats, fish, drinks, breads, cereals, dairy products, vegetables, and snacks—all preserved in protective packaging or stored in refrigerated cases and shelved neatly in a way that allows you to quickly find what you want. It is not a matter of buying "food" or not buying "food." It is a marginal decision regarding how much or how little of particular food products you wish to buy today. If the price of bibb lettuce increases even slightly you might switch to the romaine. If that is too high, you walk away from the lettuce entirely and begin an examination of the cucumbers, zucchini, and tomatoes.

Contrast the marginal decisions made by grocery shoppers in market economies to the choices offered in the old Soviet Union, which imposed a system of price controls intended to make the cost of food lower. In Moscow, the shelves of grocery stores were often empty. The lines for what supplies were available were long. Uncertainty of supplies was always present. Consumers often decided to settle for what they could get. As you might easily imagine, the limited choices and uncertainty of supplies facing people in the old Soviet Union often brought out their worst behavior: rudeness, pushing, shoving, bribery, corruption, and hoarding.

Many of our religious and political leaders resist the idea of marginal analysis. They speak in terms of "all-or-nothing" choices when it comes to decisions regarding low-income housing, protecting the environment, and providing health care to the uninsured. Economists are leery of moral formulations that compel a person or society to act implying that no sacrifice is too great and to ignore the quality and quantity of the array of choices. Economists, recognizing that all choices involve costs, are skeptical of moral imperatives.

In summary, the first contribution economic education can make to moral education is to help young people understand and apply the concepts of opportunity cost and marginal analysis to moral situations. A highly developed understanding for these ideas will help young people recognize that efforts to cloud decisions with emotional appeals can produce outcomes that are neither efficient nor moral.

Myths about Economics Values

What values are inherent in the study of economics? While we regard this question as being fundamentally important, we would like to defer that discussion a little while longer. First, we will concentrate on what values are *not* inherent in economics by debunking the notion that economics is all about greed. Next, we will make the case for what values we think are properly understood as being enhanced by the study of economics.

Many people think of economics as little more than the study of greed. The profit motive, a key incentive in a market system, is regarded by some as the most concrete expression of that greed. Greed, of course, is not regarded as a virtue. It brings to mind all sorts of anti-social acts. "Money grubbing," "selfish," "pushy," "deceiving," and "conniving" are a few of the long list of derogatory adjectives associated with people who are greedy. Popular films are often loaded with such images.

Economists are sometimes their own worst enemy when it comes to making the connection between the study of economics and greed. Instructors of the principles of economics courses—the very course in which social studies teachers are likely to enroll—all too often take perverse pleasure in advertising their mistaken insight that economics is all about greed. They claim that the sole reason we have food in the stores, credit at the banks, and gas at the gas stations is because of "greedy" business people. It is hard for us to imagine getting off to a worse start in economic understanding than beginning with a focus on greed.

What is economics about if it is not about greed? The founder of economics, Adam Smith, was a moral philosopher. Smith began and ended his scholarly career with a focus on moral behavior. Smith contended that the central focus of economics is on *self-interested* behavior as contrasted with greedy or selfish behavior. The distinction between self-interested behavior and selfish behavior is important.

Adam Smith's famous statement about self-interest from the *Wealth of Nations* (1776, Book I, Chapter II) is relevant to our discussion about morality of markets. Smith argues that self-interest is natural and beneficial in making markets work well:

> It is not from the benevolence of the butcher, the brewer, or the baker, that we expect our dinner, but from their regard to their own self-interest. We address ourselves, not to their humanity but to their self-love, and never talk to them of our own necessities but of their advantages.

Paul Heyne (1994) has often used an example that we find compelling on the distinction between self-interest and selfishness. Heyne reminds us that in 1979 Mother Teresa received the Nobel Prize for Peace. Mother Teresa, a Catholic nun, was offered the $190,000 that accompanied the prize. Would Mother Teresa, a woman known for her tireless work to ease the plight of Calcutta's poor and her firm commitment to keeping her vow of poverty, accept the money? Of course she did. Was her willingness to accept the money an act of selfishness and greed? Of course not. Mother Teresa accepted the money and used it to construct a hospital for leprosy patients.

Smith would regard Mother Teresa's decision as one made in regard to her own self-interest. Mother Teresa gained much satisfaction in her work with the poor. When she was given an opportunity to help even more as a result of receiving $190,000, she took advantage of it. In this sense, her actions were both generous and self-interested. We know that many people often act as they do so as to obtain money. Yet, knowing that people respond positively to opportunities to earn money reveals little about people's character. Saints and sinners alike are interested in money.

Consider another form of self-interested behavior. Most individuals get satisfaction from caring for and helping others. You may very well give help to others because doing so makes you feel better about yourself. You may, however, care for and help an elderly parent or family member more than someone you do not know at all. This differing attitude on your part does not mean that you do not care for others or are necessarily selfish. It does mean that given your limited resources of time and energy to devote to others, you choose first to give to those closest to you, like family and friends. This is an economic choice. It means you allocate your scarce resources so as to maximize the benefit you get from it. It does not mean you are selfish.

The Absence of Markets and Immoral Behavior

Economists often comment on the contributions of market systems to encourage cooperation and courteous behavior. They stress that it is the absence of markets that tends to bring out uncooperative and rude behavior, not the presence of markets.

Here is a simple example. For years, passengers and flight attendants have complained about the uncooperative and rude behavior of airline passengers. It seems that almost all air travelers are trying to smuggle on board more bags than are permitted or are dragging on oversized bags. The same travelers who moments earlier kissed their loved ones goodbye, are transformed into unreserved warriors in the battle of the overhead bins.

The battle begins in the gate where air travelers elbow their way to the front of the line to board the aircraft as soon as possible in order to grab an overhead bin. Once on the aircraft, the real fight begins. Some passengers with seats in the rear of the plane toss their bags into the front compartments to be sure they get a spot. People with oversized bags cram them into the narrow bins, pushing the bags, coats, and hats of passengers with correctly sized luggage into the corners. People ask for help from the flight attendants but their pleas are ignored. The flight attendants say they are too short staffed to handle passenger disagreements concerning bags. Losers are left standing with their "homeless" bags. The bag chaos causes the flight to be delayed as things are sorted out. It gets worse. The excess bags people bring on pose safety risks to other passengers. Overhead bins can be dangerous if they pop open during takeoff and landing.

Are people just selfish and rude? Most economists say no, they are just responding to the absence of market incentives. The overhead bins are a commons. It's Dodge City. Nobody "owns" the space in the overhead bins. People can't trust strangers to act with cooperation or courtesy. The result is "warfare."

Things could be different. Creating an overhead bin market would bring out the best of people. Here is how. Most of today's airlines charge people extra to check a bag and offer the overhead bins for "free." It should be just the reverse. People should be charged a rental fee for the overhead compartment above their seat and be allowed to check their bags at no cost. Charging rental fees would create an overhead bins market by defining and enforcing individual ownership rights. So, business travelers—people in a hurry to see clients and not spend time waiting for bags—would be willing to pay the extra amount and would feel more secure knowing that their bin space would be waiting for them when they arrived onto the aircraft. No need to push or shove. Tourist travelers would happily check their bags knowing that they are saving money. They would have an incentive to just bring on board what they need for the flight—a book or a notebook computer. Cooperation and courtesy would be the order of the day.

It was not the presence of markets but rather the absence of markets that contributed substantially to the human suffering of the last century. Gerald Scully (1997), for example, studied the human cost in the last century resulting from widespread experimentation with socialism and communism. Scully reports that communist states killed millions of their own people in the twentieth century, far more than killed by the Nazis.

- The Soviet Union killed 54.7 million between 1917 and 1987.
- China killed 35.6 million between 1949 and 1987.
- The Khmer Rouge killed three million between 1975 and 1979 (one-third of the population of Cambodia).

It may well be the case that economic freedom is simply a part of human nature. Vladimir Lenin knew full well that the goals of the communist revolution could not be attained without the use of terror. Lenin recognized that the government would have to seize the farm-land of tens of millions of peasants. He tried during the Russian Civil War of 1918–1920 but decided to retreat leaving five million famine deaths in his wake. Joseph Stalin completed the job, however, sending millions of more affluent peasants to Siberian slave labor camps and starving the rest.

We have had several opportunities to observe first-hand the situation in Central and Eastern Europe shortly after the collapse of communism. Some observations such as the widespread poverty and destruction of the environment were obvious. But, there was grave moral damage as well. In Russia and parts of Eastern Europe, we witnessed the deep-seated and widespread cynicism that breeds corruption. There was a sense, for example, that you could trust no one who was not a family member or a loyal friend. If you were traveling, you depended on family or personal contacts to get what you needed. Strangers could not be trusted. Strangers might steal from you, charge exorbitant prices for shoddy merchandise, or worse. Doing business with strangers was nearly impossible. In a system where contracts were routinely violated, promises were useless. Honesty between strangers counted for nothing.

Communism depended on coercion and terror to get people to produce the goods and services desired by the regime. Successful cooperation with the government opened the doors to good schools, better apartments, power, freedom to travel, and access to stores that had products from the West. Failure to cooperate resulted in limited opportunities, demotion, threats, exile, or death.

In market systems, people do business with strangers all the time. While markets are not perfect, people buy and sell goods and services from strangers and travel with relatively few worries about safety. In market systems, people cooperate by choice—not because they are saints but because it is in their self-interest to do so. There is no need for elaborate government-enforced rewards and sanctions of the sort that were once routine in the former Soviet Union.

Morality of Markets for the Conscience

At long last, we now turn to the topic of what *are* the values inherent in economics. From Smith's time until now, we recognize that market systems foster the development of positive values in people. This is due to the competitive, profit-oriented nature of the private sector. To some of our readers, this might seem to be an unusual claim. Perhaps an example might help.

Imagine that you are the manager of the Big Red Discount Store, and you want to hire a new worker in the food-service department to manage the popcorn concession.

- You will pay the worker $10.00 an hour.
- You charge customers $1.20 for a bag of popcorn.
- After deducting the cost of the popcorn, you will have $1.00 left over to pay the worker and earn a profit.
- Your accountant tells you that new workers must make and sell an average of ten bags an hour for the popcorn concession to break even.

You have two candidates for the job. Which candidate will you hire?

- A man of the same race and age as you who can make and sell eight bags of popcorn an hour?
- An older woman whose ethnic background is clearly different from yours and who can make and sell 20 bags an hour?

If your goal is to maximize profits, you will accomplish this by hiring the worker who makes and sells 20 bags an hour. To the profit-motivated manager, it is profit—not race, age, or gender—that provides a basis for decision-making. In general, businesses that are run for profit have an incentive to hire the most productive workers regardless of race, gender, age, religion, or sexual orientation.

Unfettered markets tend to reward productivity and discourage discrimination. Gorman (2008) points out that those problems arise when government steps in to protect the bigots against competition. This was the case in the United States with the passage of the Jim Crow laws in the late nineteenth and early twentieth centuries. It was also the case in South Africa when mine owners attempted to lay off high-priced white workers in order to hire lower-priced black workers. Higher-paying jobs were eventually reserved for whites only after white workers successfully persuaded the government to place extreme restrictions on blacks' abilities to work through apartheid.

Market systems provide strong incentives that encourage ethical behavior. We are indebted to Dierdre McCloskey, who has influenced our thinking in this regard. McCloskey argues that the growth of markets has expanded virtue, not vice. She states (1994, p. 181):

> I am suggesting, in other words, that we stop sneering at the bourgeoisie, stop being ashamed of being middle class and stop defining a participant in an economy as an amoral brute. The bad talk creates reality. Adam Smith knew that a capitalist society such as eighteenth-century Edinburgh could not flourish without the virtues of trustworthiness or bourgeois pride, supported by talk. Smith's other book, *The Theory of Moral Sentiments*, which scarcely an economist reads, was about love, not greed; esteem, not venality. Yet, even economists have learned by now that moral sentiment must ground a market.

McCloskey has identified a list of what she calls bourgeois virtues. We have added and subtracted from McCloskey's initial list. Among the positive values associated with economics and commerce are discipline, honesty, trustworthiness, tolerance, cooperation, courtesy, enterprise, thrift, and responsibility. Table 5.1 explains these values by contrasting market-oriented values to non-market-oriented values. Market values are those encouraged in market economies. Non-market values are those encouraged in command or traditional economies.

Private Property and Values

The foundation of a market economy that supports moral values is the principle of private property rights. Free markets may be viewed as morally superior to other forms of economic organization because they are based on voluntary relationships (rather than force) and respect for both private property and the sanctity of the individual. This respect lies at the heart of America's founding rights. Freedom's first principle holds that each person owns himself. Therefore, slavery, murder, and rape are unjust because they are violations of private property, just as theft is a violation of private property. Since it is wrong and unlawful to take or destroy property of another without the owner's permission, individuals must engage in voluntary exchange to acquire the goods and services they desire. This means that the structure of the market economy requires that we serve the needs of others in order to receive the resources we use to fulfill our own needs. Individuals have many and varied needs, needs both material and spiritual. Business people and religious leaders alike can only obtain "customers" through competition. For example, both the Reverend Billy Graham and Ray Kroc (founder of McDonald's) served the needs of others in profound ways. Both stood the market test of voluntary exchange.

Implications for Teaching Economics

An idea for teaching economics in high school would be to stress the notion that market systems can actually shape positive values. The stress of market systems on self-interested behavior encourages individuals in business to pay attention to the interests of others. Business people can only be successful over the long term by identifying and producing goods and services desired by their customers. This attention to the needs of others is an important message for adolescents who seemingly believe the world revolves around them. Markets stress how honesty, tolerance, cooperation, courtesy, enterprise, thrift, and responsibility are not only worthy values; they are exactly the business practices that are rewarded in a market economy.

American history is filled with well-known and not so well-known examples of individuals who studied what it was that other people wanted and found ways to provide it to them.

Table 5.1 Market Values Versus Non-Market Values

MARKET VALUES

Discipline: Market systems—with stress on self-interested behavior—encourage individuals to discipline themselves to produce the goods and services others want. Producing the goods and services demanded by others is rewarded through income and profits.

Honesty and trustworthiness: While market systems are susceptible to occasional scams and schemes, most business people recognize that being honest and trustworthy with their customers will benefit the business over the long term. Customers will not continue to buy goods and services from people who cheat and lie to them.

Tolerance: Market systems tend to reward people who make good business decisions rather than decisions based on prejudice regarding race, religion, gender, sexual orientation, and so forth. Judging workers on merit and selling to all customers who wish to buy are practices that are rewarded in the marketplace.

Cooperation: Cooperation is seldom stressed as a basic characteristic of a market system in the same way that people most of the time ignore that oxygen is a fundamental element of their world. Market systems require vast amounts of voluntary cooperation that produce extraordinary results that we regard as ordinary. For example, how does a car with parts from ten countries, hundreds of suppliers, and thousands of distributors, come to be sold in towns the size of cornfields? The act of producing and distributing cars requires an almost unimaginable amount of cooperation among strangers.

NON-MARKET VALUES

Discipline: Non-market systems depend on tradition or force to encourage individuals to produce the goods and services desired by others. Failure to produce can lead to loss of respect, misery, or worse.

Honesty and trustworthiness: Non-market systems rely on tradition or force to encourage individuals to be honest and trustworthy. Since this is hard to enforce, people over the long term tend to trust only family and friends. It is hard to maintain business relationships when there are no sanctions enforced by consumers.

TOLERANCE: Non-market systems rely on tradition or force to encourage individuals to be tolerant. This is hard to enforce. Intolerance tends to lurk just beneath the surface of many human interactions. Hate is unleashed as soon as external forces are removed. Witness the strife in parts of Africa.

Cooperation: Non-market systems rely on tradition or force to encourage individuals to work together. Chairman Stalin, for example, deliberately distributed different forms of manufacturing and agriculture across the former Soviet Union to force people of different ethnic backgrounds to cooperate with each other. As soon as the threat of force was removed under Chairman Gorbachev, it all collapsed. Cooperation brought about by coercion could not be sustained.

Courtesy: Market systems encourage people to be courteous as a means of doing business. Customers, for example, are not likely to favor business people who are rude. While imperfect, over the long term civil behavior tends to be rewarded. Consumers in market systems expect to be treated with dignity and respect. "How may I help you?" delivered with a smile is rewarded.

Enterprise: Market systems promise large rewards for entrepreneurs. Risk and change are materially rewarded. New goods and services constantly appear while others fade away.

Thrift: Market systems tend to reward people who save and live below their means. These, among other things, are the characteristics of people who become wealthy in market systems. Thrift also helps fulfill the needs of others. By saving and accumulating capital, individuals earn interest. This is true because income is lent to others to fulfill their needs and creates more jobs, more wealth, and an improved standard of living.

Responsibility: Market systems—with the emphasis on self-interested behavior—tend to focus on the individual and individual actions. The threat of failure is sobering and it tends to encourage individuals to take responsibility for their actions. Market systems also tend to reward people who make good business decisions.

Courtesy: Non-market systems rely on tradition or force to encourage individuals to be courteous. Indifferences or antipathy toward customers is a persistent problem. Think of the long lines at your Department of Motor Vehicles. Remember the last time a government clerk closed his or her service line because it was break time. We recall that security guards in the former Soviet Union were often assigned to each floor in Moscow department stores. The guards were not there to protect against thieves. They were there to protect the store clerks from angry customers.

Enterprise: Non-market systems tend to reward behavior that is in line with the rules. "Follow the manual" might be the motto. Following the manual rarely results in inventions and innovations that materially improve our standard of living.

Thrift: Little is to be gained in non-market systems by saving. Individuals can never be certain when anyone, from the village leaders to the government, might appropriate an individual's wealth. This is not as farfetched as it might seem. Remember how Argentina nationalized the bank accounts of its citizens in order to help the government pay down international debts. In non-market systems, saving is not its own reward.

Responsibility: Non-market systems rely on tradition or force to encourage individuals to act responsibly. Shirking is often respected. The culture calls for putting in your time and waiting it out for early retirement. People who are caught doing their jobs are regarded as not being clever enough to keep their heads down to protect themselves, their family, and their buddies.

- Commodore Vanderbilt made innovations in shipping industry and made shipping and travel cheaper and faster for customers.
- John D. Rockefeller revolutionized the worldwide production of oil, making it possible for common people to afford inexpensive lighting for their home at night, thus enabling a family life to people who worked all day.
- Sam Walton changed the life in small-town America by offering great retail products and a huge selection at low prices.

The list is long of people who improved the lives of consumers by acting in their own self-interest. Anna and Melville Bissell brought us the carpet cleaner. Alfred Fuller sold Fuller Brushes door to door. William Colgate helped Americans clean up their acts with his soap products. Perhaps the experiences of such individuals could be used as examples to teach about the virtues associated with markets and economics.

There is a set of curriculum materials produced by the Council on Economic Education designed to teach specifically about the ethics of markets. *Teaching the Ethical Foundations of Economics* contains ten lessons that introduce an ethical dimension to economics in the tradition of Adam Smith. This curriculum stresses the role ethics and character play in a market economy and how, in turn, markets influence ethical behavior. Table 5.2 presents the table of contents of this curriculum.

Conclusion

We wonder whether it might be possible to reform the teaching of economics to stress the importance of values of the market place. How could an economics curriculum be modified to develop the self-control, industry, and gentleness valued by such moral philosophers as Adam Smith and David Hume? Exhortation regarding values is not enough. We think classes might be modified to show how the concepts of opportunity cost and marginal analysis can help students come to understand that self-interested behavior can be channeled to

Table 5.2 Teaching the Ethical Foundations of Economics: Table of Ccontents

LESSON 1—DOES SCIENCE NEED ETHICS?
In this lesson the students see how biases may enter into the discovery of facts.

LESSON 2—WHAT IS THE DIFFERENCE BETWEEN SELF-INTEREST AND GREED?
In this lesson the students first explore the concepts of greed and self-interest through a class discussion. In pairs, they play a famous game in economics and ethics: the Ultimatum Game.

LESSON 3—DO MARKETS NEED ETHICAL STANDARDS?
The students participate in an exercise that demonstrates the motives of self-interest, duty, and character in economic transactions.

LESSON 4—DO MARKETS MAKE US MORE MORAL?
In this lesson the students discuss situations that demonstrate how markets reward moral behavior.

LESSON 5—WHAT ARE THE MORAL LIMITS OF MARKETS?
The lesson begins with the students brainstorming ways to allocate a scarce good within a small group. Then they evaluate market and non-market mechanisms for allocating goods and services. This leads to a discussion of the moral limits of markets.

LESSON 6—WHAT SHOULD WE DO ABOUT SWEATSHOPS?
This lesson introduces the students to three main ways of analyzing moral problems. The students apply these approaches to evaluate sweatshops.

LESSON 7—SHOULD WE ALLOW A MARKET FOR TRANSPLANT ORGANS?
The students learn that there is a shortage of transplant organs in the United States. They explore ways to reduce the shortage, particularly by increasing the supply.

LESSON 8—IS EFFICIENCY AN ETHICAL CONCEPT?
In this lesson, the students discover how goals and value judgments affect decisions about efficiency and welfare. They also learn how economists measure efficiency.

LESSON 9—DO BUSINESSES HAVE A SOCIAL RESPONSIBILITY?
The students read two viewpoints on the social responsibility of business from Milton Friedman, a Nobel laureate in economics, and John Mackey, founder of Whole Foods Market.

LESSON 10—WHAT IS ECONOMIC JUSTICE?
In this lesson, the students explore basic ideas of justice through a class discussion. Then they play the Veil of Ignorance game.

produce socially beneficial behavior. Making significant distinctions between the concepts of greed and self-interest would be a valuable start as well as an understanding that selfishness and self-interest are different. Perhaps economics students could come to grasp that people who work in the private sector—the most likely people being their parents and other members of their families—may be contributing to the social good while pursuing their self-interest and that of their families.

References

Gorman, L. (2008). Discrimination. In D.R. Henderson (Ed.) *The concise encyclopedia of economics.* Indianapolis: Liberty Fund.

Heyne, P. (1994). *The economic way of thinking.* New York: Macmillan College Publishing Company.

McCloskey D.N. (1994). Bourgeois virtue. *American Scholar* (63) 2, 177–191.

Morton, J.S. and Wight, J.B. (2003). *Teaching the ethical foundations of economics.* New York: National Council on Economic Education.

Scully, G.W. (1997). *Murder by the state.* Dallas: National Center for Policy Analysis.

Smith, A. (1976 [1776]). *An inquiry into the nature and causes of the wealth of nations.* New York: Oxford University Press.

PART II

MAKING ECONOMICS COOL IN SCHOOL

6

A CHALLENGING ASSIGNMENT IN TROUBLED TIMES

What Every First Year High School Economics Teacher Needs to Know

Jane S. Lopus

For many high school social studies teachers, being assigned to teach economics is like a bad dream come true. Add in the financial meltdown of 2008–2009, and it only gets worse. Teachers who have majored in history or political science generally expect to be assigned to teach these subjects because they are their areas of expertise. They are often surprised to be assigned to teach economics and to find out that they are considered qualified to do so. Although many social science teachers feel comfortable teaching a variety of courses such as geography, world history, and U.S. history and government, the subject matter of economics often does not fall into this comfort zone.

As bad as an economics teaching assignment might seem to a social studies teacher in normal times, recent times have been anything but normal. The U.S. economy suffered through its worst economic downturn since the Great Depression. "What to teach" might seem unclear, as a 1990s consensus about the economy as a whole unraveled (Niederjohn and Wood, 2009). Even in the best of times, economics is perceived as being abstract, difficult, mathematical, and irrelevant—in short, the dismal science.[1]

If teachers studied economics in high school or college but had a negative experience, they are unlikely to look forward to teaching it to others. A different problem may arise for teachers who have majored in economics in college. These teachers likely feel comfortable with the subject matter, but wonder whether recent developments have made their knowledge obsolete. Further, they may be at a loss as to how to break down complex or mathematical concepts to make

97

the subject relevant and comprehensible for high school students. University economics classes largely rely on "chalk and talk" methodology. Relying on this methodology in the high school classroom could result in disengaged and bored students who quickly lose interest in the subject.

To those teaching high school economics for the first time, we who have been involved in high school economics offer the following reassurance: there is help available. If you seek out this help, and with some effort on your part, you can do a great job teaching high school economics and the experience can be enjoyable and rewarding for both you and your students. Beyond that, recent economic turmoil has not changed the basic principles of economics and in fact has provided fresh new examples. In this chapter, we outline suggestions for you as a first-year high school economics teacher, whether you are a new teacher or a teacher with experience teaching other subjects. Our recommendations come from personal experience teaching high school economics, from working with high school economics teachers in professional development situations, and from talking to national leaders in economic education at the high school level. We organize our advice into a list of 12 suggestions addressing areas of content, methodology, materials, and professional development.

Twelve Suggestions for First-Year High School Economics Teachers

Teaching the Content

1. Focus on economics as a way of thinking. John Maynard Keynes said, "The theory of economics does not furnish a body of settled conclusions immediately applicable to policy. It is a method rather than a doctrine, an apparatus of the mind, a technique which helps its possessor to draw correct conclusions." As this quotation aptly points out, economics *is* a way of thinking and a decision-making process. Every decision is, in fact, an economic decision. When you have to make a choice, you give something up, and what you give up is the opportunity cost of your decision. Thus every choice has a cost. This straightforward idea has many applications to the daily lives of high school students. If they choose to get an after-school job, what is the opportunity cost? If they choose to attend the state university after graduation, what is the opportunity cost? Weighing these opportunity costs against the benefits of the decision leads to rational decision-making. Economics can be defined as the science of making choices, and this definition emphasizes the importance of learning to make good decisions.

Recent economic turbulence does not change any of this. If anything, it increases the importance of making good decisions. Economists make decisions by weighing benefits and costs, on the margin. The point is not to teach students about right or wrong decisions, but rather about using the analytical tools of economic decision-making correctly. Marginal analysis involves looking at effects of decisions involving additional units of something. What are the (opportunity) costs and benefits of studying economics for one more hour? Of the school eliminating a sports program? Of the government spending more money on health care? Students often find this process to be exhilarating as they learn to assess opportunity costs and apply economic thinking to their own lives and to events they hear about in the news.

To teach economic decision-making or economic reasoning, consider using the six-step "Guide to Economic Reasoning," formerly called "The Handy-Dandy Guide" (*Capstone*, NCEE 2003a), reproduced as Table 6.1.

Table 6.1 The Guide to Economic Reasoning

1. *People choose.* People choose the alternative that seems best to them because it involves the least cost and the greatest benefit. People economize.

2. *People's choices involve costs—monetary costs and opportunity costs.* Opportunity cost is the second-best alternative people give up in making a choice.

3. *People respond to incentives in predictable ways.* Incentives are benefits or rewards that encourage people to act. When incentives change, people's choices change.

4. *People create economic systems and these systems influence incentives and people's choices.* How people cooperate is governed by written and unwritten rules. As rules change, incentives change and choices change.

5. *People gain when they trade voluntarily.* People can produce more with given resources by concentrating on what they do best. They can trade the goods or services they produce for other valuable goods or services.

6. *People's choices have consequences that lie in the future.* The important costs and benefits in economic decisions are those that will appear in the future. Economics stresses the importance of making choices about the future. People cannot choose to change the past.

Table 6.2 The Voluntary National Content Standards in Economics

1. Productive resources are limited. Therefore, people cannot have all the goods and services they want; as a result, they must choose some things and give up others.

2. Effective decision-making requires comparing the additional costs of alternative with the additional benefits. Most choices involve doing a little more or a little less of something; few choices are all-or-nothing decisions.

3. Different methods can be used to allocate goods and services. People, acting individually or collectively through government, must choose which methods to use to allocate different kinds of goods and services.

4. People respond predictably to positive and negative incentives.

5. Voluntary exchange occurs only when all participating parties expect to gain. This is true for trade among individuals or organizations within a nation, and among individuals or organizations in different nations.

6. When individuals, regions, and nations specialize in what they can produce at the lowest cost and then trade with others, both production and consumption increase.

7. Markets exist when buyers and sellers interact. This interaction determines market prices and thereby allocates scarce goods and services.

8. Prices send signals and provide incentives to buyers and sellers. When supply or demand changes, market prices adjust, affecting incentives.

9. Competition among sellers lowers costs and prices, and encourages producers to produce more of what consumers are willing and able to buy. Competition among buyers increases prices and allocates goods and services to those people who are willing and able to pay the most for them.

10. Institutions evolve in market economies to help individuals and groups accomplish their goals. Banks, labor unions, corporations, legal systems, and not-for-profit organizations are examples of important institutions. A different kind of institution, clearly defined and well enforced property rights, is essential to a market economy.

11. Money makes it easier to trade, borrow, save, invest, and compare the value of goods and services.

12. Interest rates, adjusted for inflation, rise and fall to balance the amount saved with the amount borrowed, thus affecting the allocation of scarce resources between present and future uses.

13. Income for most people is determined by the market value of the productive resources they sell. What workers earn depends, primarily, on the market value of what they produce and how productive they are.

14. Entrepreneurs are people who take the risks of organizing productive resources to make goods and services. Profit is an important incentive that leads entrepreneurs to accept the risks of business failure.

15. Investment in factories, machinery, new technology, and the health, education, and training of people can raise future standards of living.

16. There is an economic role for government to play in a market economy whenever the benefits of a government policy outweigh its costs. Governments often provide for national defense, address environmental concerns, define and protect property rights, and attempt to make markets more competitive. Most government policies also redistribute income.

17. Costs of government policies sometimes exceed benefits. This may occur because of incentives facing voters, government officials, and government employees, because of actions by special interest groups that can impose costs on the general public, or because social goals other than economic efficiency are being pursued.

18. A nation's overall levels of income, employment, and prices are determined by the interaction of spending and production decisions made by all households, firms, government agencies, and others in the economy.

19. Unemployment imposes costs on individuals and nations. Unexpected inflation imposes costs on many people and benefits some others because it arbitrarily redistributes purchasing power. Inflation can reduce the rate of growth of national living standards, because individuals and organizations use resources to protect themselves against the uncertainly of future prices.

20. Federal government budgetary policy and the Federal Reserve System's monetary policy influence the overall levels of employment, output, and prices.

Source: NCEE (1997).

5. Use current events to make economics relevant. This will keep materials alive for both your students and you. You can provide examples and applications of economic concepts using current issues and topics. Every month a wealth of economic information is distributed by government agencies. Newspapers report on these and you can use the recent data in them to update the content in textbooks. Especially in times of economic turbulence, inflation and unemployment rates as well as monetary policy announcements can make interesting topics for your course. Make a habit of keeping up with the economic information in the news and encourage your students to do the same. Introduce your students to quality media sources and emphasize the importance of economics in understanding the world.

6. Give careful consideration to the role of personal finance. Many schools and districts consider personal finance to be an important component of a high school economics class, and major high school textbooks generally include sections on related topics. Some personal finance materials (such as those available from the Council for Economic Education, www.councilforeconed.org, formerly the National Council on Economic Education, NCEE) attempt to frame personal finance decisions into the economic way of thinking against economic concepts such as scarcity and opportunity costs.

Some instructors find that a stock market simulation can enhance student interest, teach students first-hand about investments, and

Table 6.3 Sample Outline of a One-semester High School Economics Course

---

1. Introduction to economics and economic systems (2 weeks)
Major economic concepts: Scarcity, opportunity costs, decision-making, incentives, market economic system, command economic system, traditional economic system, economic institutions.

2. Markets, supply, and demand (3 weeks)
Major economic concepts: Markets and prices, supply and demand, controls on prices.

3. Business, labor, and market structure (3 weeks)
Major economic concepts: Productivity, profit, competition, monopoly, entrepreneurs, forms of business organizations, stock market, labor unions, income, human capital.

4. The role of government (2 weeks)
Major economic concepts: Role of government in a market-based economic system, market failures, government failures.

5. Macroeconomics (5 weeks)
Major economic concepts: Gross domestic product, investment, unemployment, money, interest rates, inflation and deflation, Federal Reserve, monetary policy, fiscal policy, national debt.

6. The world economy (3 weeks)
Major economic concepts: Comparative advantage, voluntary trade/exchange, barriers to trade, exchange rates, trade deficits and surpluses, international organizations.

Source: Adapted from "Sample Outline of a One-Semester High School Course in Economics," NCEE (1985).

encourage students to follow current events. There were many teaching opportunities in the stock market's steep falloff in early 2009, its quick recovery of value later in 2009, and the continuing volatility that followed. A variety of games and simulations are available on the Internet or through your local center for economic education. If you choose to have your students participate in a stock market simulation, we would caution you about allowing this element to become too large as a portion of your academic program. Personal investing education can play an important role in your economics course, but there is an opportunity cost in terms of instruction lost on other topics.

Methodology for Teaching High School Economics

7. *Use activity-based lessons.* Active learning will both enliven your instruction and facilitate student understanding. There is no need to teach high school economics solely through lectures because there are many ways to actively involve students and make economics come

alive for them. Lessons available through the Council for Economic Education focus on activity-based learning. *Economics in Action: 14 Greatest Hits for Teaching High School Economics* (NCEE 2003b) is a best seller in this category and a good place to start. The lessons in this volume introduce a variety of decision-making skills and economic concepts using simulations, role-plays, group decision-making, problem-solving, classroom demonstrations, and group presentations. For example, if you are looking for a lesson on supply and demand, you may wish to begin with Lesson 7, "A Market in Wheat." This lesson has students act as buyers and sellers to determine an equilibrium price. The supply and demand diagram evolves from the simulation. If you are looking for an intuitive way to teach about comparative advantage, consider using Lesson 13, "Comparative Advantage and Trade in a Global Economy." Here students discover the difference between absolute and comparative advantage through a role-play with Bert and Betsy, a brother and sister who have to complete household chores before they can go out with their friends. Although changing to an active teaching style may be uncomfortable at first, you will learn by doing and so will your students.

Materials for Teaching High School Economics

8. Use one of the many good high school economics textbooks available. Using a good high school textbook can help to structure your course and the course content. Many high school economics texts are written by university professors who have also written college-level textbooks. A recent survey of the existing high school textbooks (Leet and Lopus, 2007) found more similarities than differences among most of the textbooks, although there were differences in content emphasis. Some teachers chose to use college-level textbooks, which are obviously appropriate for Advanced Placement economics classes. For other classes, using a good high school-level textbook can give students a guide to the material that will be covered and provide examples and information to supplement activities covered in class.

9. Take advantage of the many good supplementary materials available for teaching economics. Materials published by the Council for Economic Education have been mentioned earlier but deserve emphasis here. A quick perusal of the Council's online catalog (http://store.councilforeconed.org) will reveal a wide variety of teacher-friendly materials. Other excellent supplementary materials are available through regional Federal Reserve Banks and other scholarly organizations. Current economic data are available from many government sources such as the Bureau of Economic Analysis and the Bureau of Labor Statistics. The Federal Reserve Bank of St. Louis maintains an easy-to-use searchable database of economic data called FRED (http://research.stlouisfed.org/fred2). With up-to-date data, you can transform economic turbulence into a teaching opportunity.

Professional Development, Formal and Informal

10. Obtain copies of mainstream college-level principles textbooks in both microeconomics and macroeconomics. These books can serve as a valuable reference for you and will allow you to look up concepts, develop background knowledge, and learn new examples and applications. If you understand the material at one step above the high school level, you will be in a better position to explain the concepts to your students. Professors at local colleges and universities often receive many free sample textbooks and may be willing to give them to you. Or you may buy used copies at reasonable prices.

11. Find a mentor. Don't be afraid to ask for help: all economics teachers were first-year teachers at one time. If you are lucky, there will be an experienced, accomplished economics teacher in your school or district willing to help you get started. If not, attending regional professional development workshops will put you in touch with economics teachers from other schools and districts. Finding a mentor will make you feel less isolated if you are the only one teaching economics in your school. There are several professional sources for locating people to help and guide you. The Council for Economic Education has a network of state councils and university-based Centers for Economic Education dedicated to helping K–12 teachers with economics. Join the Global Association of Economics Teachers (GATE: www.councilforeconed/gate). GATE maintains an active discussion board where your fellow teachers can answer your questions and offer advice. Even if your mentor is an online advisor, knowing who you can go to for help can be a great confidence builder.

12. Participate in professional development programs in economics. These programs may be offered by your state Council for Economic Education or your local Center for Economic Education, by your regional Federal Reserve Bank, or through other professional organizations. Consider attending the Council for Economic Education's annual conference, held in conjunction with the National Association of Economic Educators and GATE. Also consider attending economics sessions at the annual conference of the National Council for the Social Studies or your state Council for the Social Studies. Any chance you have to network with others interested in teaching high school economics is a chance to expand your expertise in this field. You can also bring your knowledge up to date by attending sessions at these conferences.

Conclusion

Although teaching economics for the first time can seem like a daunting challenge, we hope we have convinced you that the content is manageable and relevant. There are great materials available to help you take an activity-based learning approach. There are people and organizations willing and ready to help. Troubled economic times, in addition to being a challenge, also provide opportunities to bring in current events and new examples. Once you get started, you may join a growing group of teachers who enter the economics classroom with reservations and trepidation but quickly find that economics is their favorite subject to teach—and a favorite of their students. Our last bit of advice is to enjoy the challenge and have fun.

Acknowledgments

I would like to thank Bruce Damasio, Don Fortner, Sally Meek, and Sandra Wright for great ideas and suggestions. All have served as Presidents of GATE. I would also like to thank Don Leet for helpful comments.

Note

1. The term "dismal science" was likely first used by Thomas Carlyle to describe economics in 1849, but is often associated with Thomas Malthus's *An Essay on the Principle of Population* (1798), where the world's population is predicted to grow faster than the food supply.

References

Leet, D.R. and Lopus, J.S. (2007). Ten observations on high school economics textbooks. *Citizenship, Social and Economics Education: An International Journal*, 7(3), 201–214.

National Council on Economic Education. (2003a). *Capstone: Exemplary lessons for high school economics*. New York: National Council on Economic Education.

National Council on Economic Education. (2003b). *Economics in action: 14 greatest hits for teaching high school economics*. New York: National Council on Economic Education.

National Council on Economic Education. (1997). *Voluntary national content standards in economics*. New York: National Council on Economic Education.

National Council on Economic Education. (1985). *Master curriculum guide in economics, teaching strategies: high school economics course*. New York: National Council on Economic Education.

Niederjohn, M.S. and Wood, W.C. (2009). Keynesian, monetarist and supply-side policies: An old debate gets new life. *Social Education*, 73(2), 68–70.

Walstad, W.B. and Rebeck, K. (2001). *Test of economic literacy, third edition examiner's manual*. New York: National Council on Economic Education.

7

A JEWEL FOR YOUR SCHOOL'S CURRICULUM IN UNCERTAIN ECONOMIC TIMES

The Advanced Placement Economics Course

John Morton

The confident prosperity of the early 2000s has given way to economic uncertainty, including doubt about the economy's future course and reservations about economists' models to fully capture the changed environment. Is this a good time to be adding a challenging teaching and learning assignment, in the form of college-level economics instruction in high school? This chapter argues that the answer is "yes," with Advanced Placement (AP) Economics holding substantial promise for teaching and learning.

Perhaps you are an economics teacher and have been assigned to teach AP Economics next year. Or maybe your school is considering adding Advanced Placement to its economics course offerings. Or you may have been hired to teach economics and just found out that one of your courses will be at the AP level. In any of these scenarios, you realize that you're being asked to teach at a higher level than before. You realize that the structure of the economy may have recently changed in fundamental ways. Furthermore, the school administration will see your students' scores and compare them to national results. In fact, perhaps the entire world will see those scores. No one told you that you would be teaching in a fishbowl. This chapter will not only help you be more successful in teaching AP Economics but hopefully will also make teaching AP Economics your most rewarding teaching experience ever.

What Exactly Is Advanced Placement Economics?

AP Macroeconomics and AP Microeconomics are two of the 33 courses and examinations offered by The College Board. According to The College Board (2009), approximately 1.4 million students took more than 2.5 million AP exams in 2007, and about 14,000 schools worldwide have developed one or more courses that have received authorization from The College Board.

Macroeconomics and Microeconomics are separate courses and exams. The courses are representative of introductory-level college economics courses. In developing the course outlines, the AP Economics test development committee surveys the economics departments of over 200 colleges and universities. Each exam presumes one semester of college-level economics and is graded on a 1–5 scale with 5 the top score. Although individual colleges and universities decide the score required to grant credit, The College Board generally considers a 3, 4, or 5 to be a "passing" grade.

The number of AP Economics exams administered has grown rapidly. The AP Economics course debuted in 1989, and 5,781 Macro and Micro exams were administered in the initial year. In 2009, 119,459 exams were administered, a 20-fold increase. There were 3,305 schools offering AP Macro and 2,652 schools offering AP Micro. In Macro, 56.7 percent of the students "passed" the test with a 3, 4, or 5; 15.7 percent received a 5. In Micro, 65 percent of the students "passed" the test; 17.9 percent received a 5 (The College Board, 2009).

Should Your School Offer AP Economics?

The first decision a school must make is whether to offer economics at the AP level. There are several good reasons to offer AP Economics, and the economic and financial turbulence of recent years only strengthens that case. However, there are also several caveats to consider.

1. AP Economics Prepares Students for College

Much of the research shows that AP subjects prepare students for college. For example, Breland and Oltman (2001) concluded that students who received college credit for AP Economics performed in higher-level microeconomics and macroeconomics courses as well as or better than students who had earned credit in the college introductory course. A University of Texas study (Dodd et al., 2002) showed that AP students exempted from the college introductory course took as many or more class hours in the subject area and had the same or higher grades in the additional courses as students who did not take the AP course. Finally, Dougherty et al. (2006) found that after controlling for other factors, students who earned a 3 or higher on one or more AP exams in the areas of English, mathematics, science, and social studies were more likely to graduate from college in five years or fewer compared to non-AP students.

Some recent evidence, however, contradicts these studies. A study of 18,000 college students in introductory biology, chemistry, and physics found little evidence that AP courses boosted performance in the sciences. According to Philip Sadler (Bradt, 2006), one of the study's authors, "our survey, the largest ever of its type, suggests that AP courses do not contribute substantially to student success in college." The preponderance of evidence, however, shows that successful AP students do well in college.

2. AP Students Learn the Subject at a Higher Level than Students in Regular Classes

Even if it is uncertain whether AP students do better than non-AP students in some college science introductory courses, AP Economics does help students learn the subject at a higher level than students in regular courses. Because AP subjects have measurable results, teachers have an incentive to be better prepared. Although almost anything could be covered in a course called "economics," an AP Economics course must have the content and rigor of the college introductory course.

A downside of this is that an AP course is less flexible than the regular course. The more rigid curriculum might cause some instructors to teach exclusively to the test or ignore many of the ideas that make economics truly interesting. However, when economic news dominates the headlines, it is not hard to get students interested and to connect the economic news to the content of the AP course.

3. Students in Regular Economics Courses Might Benefit from the AP Economics Program

Most instructors will teach one or two sections of AP Economics and regular economics the rest of the time. The additional preparation for AP increases the quality and rigor of all the classes taught by an AP instructor. In addition, the AP teacher can be the go-to expert for other economics and social studies teachers when they need help with basic concepts or policy questions. In times of economic uncertainty, a few durable economic concepts make the news understandable to a well-prepared AP economics instructor, who can then share that knowledge with colleagues.

4. AP Economics Provides Feedback on School Success

Today, schools are being held accountable for measurable results, even as a slow economy limits the resources available for school budgets (Kalita, 2009). Voters want results when they are asked to fund public schools. Parents want to see results when they are choosing a public, charter, or private school for their children.

AP results provide valuable feedback about the success of school programs. The results are measurable by student, teacher, and school. School results can be compared to national results. At a time when education is under attack for low standards, courses such as AP Economics can make a difference in how students and parents view a school's quality and competitiveness.

5. AP Credit Saves Students Money and Makes College More Affordable

In a time of increasing financial pressure on the budgets of college-bound students' families (Korn, 2009), AP credit is the most inexpensive credit that most students can acquire. For less than $100 per exam, students can save thousands of dollars in college expenses. Equally important, having AP credits provides students more flexibility when choosing courses. It also allows students the option to carry a lighter course load when taking difficult courses or working to earn more money.

Getting Going: Preparing to Teach an Effective AP Economics Course

Before teaching a single student, instructors should take several steps in order to prepare to teach an effective course.

1. Decide Whether to Teach Macroeconomics, Microeconomics, or Both

It is very difficult to teach both AP Macroeconomics and Microeconomics in one semester. As economists know, the key is to make rational choices. In many schools offering a one-semester course, the choice is Macro. The rationale is that many states require a semester of economics and a semester of government for graduation and Macro is a better fit with government. An unstated reason may be that Macro is less mathematical than Micro.

However, a strong case can be made to teach Micro, which provides a better foundation for future economics courses than Macro. Almost every concept and analytical tool developed in a Micro course will apply to other economics courses. Also, Micro incorporates more economic thinking, which can be applied to almost any situation. Finally, some Micro must be taught for students to learn Macro so teaching Micro can be a more efficient way to cover the content in one semester.

The best idea is to teach Macro and Micro in a year-long course. Students who are successful on both the AP Macro and Micro exams can earn six hours of college credit and move directly to intermediate-level economics in college. It is also more efficient to teach Micro first because basic concepts and skills do not have to be retaught before beginning Macro. A year-long course also allows more discussion about the future prospects of today's uncertain economy.

2. Spend Time on The College Board's AP Central Website

There is a wealth of information on the AP Central website at http:// apcentral.collegeboard.com (The College Board, 2010a). The most important feature is the *Economics Course Perspective* (informally known as the "Acorn Book"), which lays out the content of the course and gives the amount of time that should be dedicated to each topic. These are not just suggestions. For example, if 10 to 15 percent of the Micro course is on supply and demand, you can be sure that 10 to 15 percent of exam questions will be on supply and demand. The test is developed from the *Economics Course Perspective*.

Next check out some of the sample course syllabi, which give ideas to help teachers construct the syllabus for their individual courses.

The website also contains past free-response questions and a practice test. In addition, released AP Macro and Micro exams along with the answers and scoring rubrics are available for sale. Taking past AP exams is a great way for students to prepare for the real exam. They will know exactly where they currently stand.

Buy the *Economics Teacher's Guide*, which contains syllabi developed by teachers who currently teach AP Economics and college professors who currently teach an introductory economics course. The guide has detailed lesson plans, teaching tips, and a list of recommended resources.

Finally, join the AP Economics discussion group (The College Board, 2010b) to gain insight and discuss problems with other AP teachers.

3. Write Your Syllabus and Submit It to The College Board for an Audit

All AP teachers must submit a syllabus to The College Board. For a new course, the deadline is the January before the fall semester begins. For existing courses, it must be resubmitted by October 15. This process intimidates many new AP teachers. It shouldn't. There are sample syllabi on the AP Central website and in the *Economics Teacher's Guide*, and each individual course syllabus will need to follow the *Economics Course Perspective*.

The audit process is actually an opportunity to plan your course in advance. Include textbook chapters, activities, and timelines in your syllabus. An AP course must stay on a tight timeline to cover all the material. AP readers (graders) often report outstanding answers to free-response questions accompanied with incomplete or nonsense answers to other questions. Probably the reason for this is that a good student took a course that failed to cover all the topics.

4. Go to an AP Economics Workshop

The College Board conducts one-day workshops that focus on AP materials, procedures, and teaching tips. These are outstanding workshops for new AP teachers. Workshop participants receive a packet that contains the *Course Perspective, Teacher's Guide*, released exams, and rubrics for the last year's free-response questions. The workshop leader, who usually is an AP reader, conducts a mock grading of some of the AP free-response questions.

In the summer, there are AP-approved workshops of longer duration. These workshops focus on content. In addition to strengthening your mastery of the economic content, these workshops will help you understand and include recent economic developments in your class. If you are unable to attend one of these workshops, try to find a Macro or Micro course that includes teaching methods. A list of approved workshops is on the AP Central website.

5. Choose a Textbook

Fortunately, most college principles of economics textbooks are similar. Choose a textbook that is compatible with your teaching style and course organization. If you are teaching only Macro or only Micro, you will find "splits," which cover only the appropriate chapters. You can find a list of textbooks as well as reviews of several on the AP Central website.

When you have narrowed your choice, be sure to tell the publishers that you will teach AP Economics. Otherwise, they may not send you a sample copy.

Also ask about ancillary materials such as student activities books, transparencies, PowerPoint slides, test banks, and teacher's manual. Many of these materials are on the publishers' websites. Effective extras can make a difference. The quality of ancillary materials should affect your choice. For example, well-written test questions can save time in test construction and ensure that the tests are reliable and valid.

6. Check out Supplementary Materials

An Internet search will reveal many resources that can be used with an AP course. These resources range from sample tests to detailed lesson plans. The Council for Economic Education (formerly National Council on Economic Education) sells an AP package that contains 55 Macro activities and 60 Micro activities in addition to lesson plans and sample test questions (Morton and Goodman, 2003).

Teaching a More Effective AP Economics Course

You want your AP Economics course to inspire your students to study more economics. If you teach just for the test or focus on technical skills, the course will not be effective. Economics is anything but the dismal science. It is more than a bundle of concepts. It is a way of thinking that helps students become more positive about their abilities and futures. The economic way of thinking relies on durable principles that, instead of changing with the economy's ups and downs, help students understand those ups and downs. Economics should help students make wiser choices and become productive. A good economics course teaches students to use cost–benefit analysis and understand that every choice has a cost. Economics helps students view life through a different set of lenses. This viewpoint offers unique insights into the seemingly chaotic confusion of human behavior. Unless this is happening, your AP course will not be all it can be.

Here are some keys to teaching a better AP Economics course:

1. Use Active Learning

With so much content to cover, a lecture approach may seem to be the way to go. It is easy to fall into the trap of having students memorize definitions, formulas, rules, and information. However, the class may be more stimulating if the students are involved in active-learning activities such as simulations, problem-solving, role playing, and group presentations. For example, if you use a double-outcry market simulation such as "A Silver Market" (Schug et al., 2003, p. 41), your students can see how market prices and quantities move toward equilibrium. After participating in this simulation, students have a deeper understanding of the supply and demand curves that follow. Two good resources for active learning lessons are *Capstone: Exemplary Lessons for High School Economics*

(Schug et al., 2003) and *Economics in Action: 14 Greatest Hits for Teaching High School Economics* (Lopus and Willis, 2003). The latter publication has simulations on market equilibrium, marginal analysis, labor productivity, effects of monetary and fiscal policies, and causes of inflation. In these activities, the students are doing, not just hearing and seeing.

2. Graph Early and Often

Students must use graphical analysis to perform well on the AP Economics examinations.

Micro uses more graphs. Students use production-possibilities graphs to illustrate scarcity, unemployment, and economic growth. They use supply and demand curves to illustrate equilibrium price and quantity, shifts in demand and supply, price ceilings and floors, consumer and producer surplus, and externalities. They study graphs to analyze product markets; they compare perfect and imperfect competition and short-run and long-run equilibrium for both the firm and the industry. Factor-market graphs include analyses of marginal revenue product and marginal physical product. Graphs are used to illustrate how wages are determined in both competitive and monopsonistic labor markets.

Macroeconomics graphs focus on aggregate demand and aggregate supply. These analyses are used in learning about inflation, deflation, and the effects of fiscal and monetary policies in both inflationary and recessionary economies. Especially because of the uncertain times, students need to be prepared for economic phenomena not now being observed—for example, high inflation that may break out in an economy currently showing price stability.

Students must understand that they are graphing behavior. If they try to memorize graphs, they will have trouble on the tests. Tell the students stories about changes in supply and demand, production-possibilities curve, perfect and imperfect competition, and aggregate supply and demand, and then have the students graph the stories.

Finally, it is essential that all graphs be clearly labeled. If the axes and lines are not labeled, students will not receive credit for their graphs on the AP exams. When you're grading your students' graphs, always point out labeling mistakes or omissions.

3. Quiz, Test, and Evaluate Your Students' Work Often

Economics builds one concept on top of another. If students do not understand the earlier concepts, they will be lost as the course progresses. The more feedback you provide, the better off your students will be.

Therefore, students need frequent assessments. Give a brief multiple-choice quiz on every chapter. These quizzes can be constructed easily from your textbook's test bank. Unit tests should include both multiple-choice and free-response questions. Multiple-choice questions should have five options as the AP tests do. Use free-response questions from previous tests, which are released each year on the AP Central website along with the scoring rubrics constructed by the AP readers. Grade the free-response questions with the scoring rubrics so the students can see how their answers will be graded. Good answers are usually succinct, but every part of the question must be answered. Students should not provide additional information that the question does not ask for. Writing an answer to an AP question is similar to an IRS audit—If they don't ask, don't tell.

4. Don't Forget Drill and Practice

Teachers often shun drill and practice, but it can be effective. Give the students multiple scenarios on production-possibilities curves, perfect competition, monopoly, aggregate supply and aggregate demand, and monetary and fiscal policies. Develop problem sets, which are difficult for students to memorize. The goal is not to cover every possible situation but rather to develop economic reasoning from constant practice. Well developed economic reasoning will then help your students to understand novel situations.

5. Emphasize Historically Weak Areas

Each year the AP Economics Chief Faculty Consultant identifies areas in which students have done poorly. This information is available on the AP Central website and should be read carefully. These topics could very well be covered in future tests.

6. Apply Economic Concepts to Current Policy Debates

Students will be more excited if they see the value of learning economics. Especially in times of economic change and uncertainty, the news brings fresh examples every day. Almost every current event can be analyzed using the economic way of thinking. Don't ignore these opportunities because you are afraid you cannot cover every topic listed in the course description. An AP Economics course must move along, but the students who have applied concepts to real events will be ahead when they face a new application on an AP Economics test.

AP teachers do their students a disservice if they ignore current economic issues in order to focus more on teaching for the test. Economics provides a unique perspective on the issues facing voters, businesses, workers, and governments. One of the major problems of the debates on policies concerning today's uncertain economic times is an ignorance of basic economic principles. A good AP course makes economic theory applicable to current problems. How do incentives affect policy choices? What are the unintended consequences of policy choices? Are open markets or government programs more effective in growing the economy? Is freer trade or protectionism more effective in growing the economy? How do scarcity and opportunity costs affect current and future government entitlement programs? How will government deficits affect short-term recovery and long-term economic growth? Not all economists will agree on the answers, but a consensus view of economists might be very different from a consensus view of politicians.

Nobel Prize-winning economist Robert Solow (2003) puts it this way:

> The usual phrase is "economic literacy," but I think that underplays what is needed: people who understand basic ideas about how the economy works, people who cannot be easily hornswoggled or snowed or diverted by lobbyists and politicians, people who are able to look at economic policy issues and realize what they are *really* about beneath the slogans. They do not have to know the answers, but they should at least understand the questions.

AP students are likely to become leaders of business, academics, and government in the future. In uncertain economic times, these leaders must understand basic economic principles.

7. Become an AP Reader

When you are an experienced AP Economics teacher, volunteer to be an AP reader (grader). There are several benefits. You will obtain unique insights as to how the free-response questions are graded. Furthermore, you will benefit from interacting with other high school and college economics instructors. One reason why the AP programs have become so successful is that AP readers create a community of teachers who value great teaching. After you are no longer a reader, you will continue to discuss approaches to teaching economics better with others dedicated to quality teaching.

Conclusion

Like economics itself, AP Economics is a positive-sum game. In a well planned and well taught course, every student can be a winner. AP Economics gives students a chance to compete at a higher level and to receive college credit at a low cost. They have the opportunity to show what they learned and compare their understanding and knowledge with a large national sample of students. But most importantly, a well taught AP Economics course provides students with tools they can use for the rest of their lives, whatever the future state of the economy. The whole is greater than the sum of its parts. When a student masters an economic way of thinking, his or her view of the world may change forever.

References

Bradt, S. (2006). High school AP courses do not predict college success in science. *Harvard University Gazette*, February 23, 2006.

Breland, H. and Oltman, P. (2001). *An analysis of Advanced Placement (AP) examinations in Economics and Comparative Government and Politics.* College Board Research Report No. 2001-4. New York: College Entrance Examination Board.

College Board, The. (2010a). AP Central. Retrieved from: http://apcentral. collegeboard.com.

College Board, The. (2010b). AP Central discussion groups. Retrieved from: http://apcentral.collegeboard.com/apc/public/homepage/7173.html.

Dodd, B., Fitzpatrick, S., DeAyala, R., and Jennings, J. (2002). *An investigation of the validity of AP grades of 3 and a comparison of AP and Non-AP student groups*. College Board Research Report 2002-9. New York: College Entrance Examination Board.

Dougherty, C., Mellor, L., and Jian, S. (2006). *The relationship between Advanced Placement and college graduation*. Austin, TX: National Center for Educational Accountability.

Kalita, S. (2009). Governors try to convince voters that budget woes are theirs, too. *Wall Street Journal*, A2. October 19, 2009.

Korn, M. (2009). A last-minute dash for tuition. *Wall Street Journal*. August 19, 2009. Retrieved from: http://online.wsj.com/article/SB10001424052 9702036747045743364200447339 80.html.

Lopus, J. and Willis, A. (2003). *Economics in action: 14 greatest hits for teaching high school economics*. New York: National Council on Economic Education.

Morton, J. and Goodman, R. (2003). *Advanced Placement Economics*. New York: National Council on Economic Education.

Schug, M. et al. (2003). *Capstone: Exemplary lessons for high school Economics*. New York: National Council on Economic Education.

Solow, R. (2003, September). *Portals*. New York: National Council on Economic Education.

8

Vital Knowledge in Troubled Times
The Role of Personal Finance in Economic Education

Michael S. Gutter and Selena Garrison

Now more than ever, financial security is linked to the choices consumers make in their personal financial management. Consumer behavior is tracked through credit bureaus and other agencies, impacting the access consumers have to loans, rental property, mobile phones, and insurance; it also impacts the cost. In addition, trends over the last several decades have transferred the risk and responsibility of funding retirement from employers to the individual as defined benefit plans have been replaced with defined contribution plans. Individuals need to decide not only to invest, but also how much and where they should invest for their retirement. In a time when financial markets show extreme year-to-year swings, the consequences of poor investment choices may be substantial (VanDerhei, 2009).

Financial markets have also become increasingly sophisticated. Deregulation has blurred the lines between banks, credit unions, and other financial institutions. The role of consumer information has increased and there is a great deal of information asymmetry between financial services providers and many consumers. Products have evolved substantially. The last several decades have seen new insurance products and securities—not to mention the influence of technology on access to information, sophistication of analysis, market functionality, and more.

Economic education has been changing over the past few decades. Influential officials such as Alan Greenspan and Ben Bernanke have strongly advocated providing more personal finance education in school. Today, the U.S. Treasury has an Office of Financial Literacy and a Presidential Task Force on Financial Literacy. This is largely due to the fact that consumers today have to make many more individual financial decisions regarding how to save and invest. This chapter will discuss the importance of financial education, its role in the economics curriculum and identify several ideas for teaching, as well as key resources.

Making the Case for Personal Finance in Economic Education

There is evidence that financial literacy has been receiving an increased amount of attention in public schools (CEE, 2009). Forty-four states in the United States currently mandate standards for personal finance education. This is up from 21 states in 1998. Of those 44 states with standards on the books, 34 require the standards to be implemented. This is up from 14 in 1998. In addition, 15 states require that a personal finance course be offered, compared to zero in 1998. A total of 13 states require that a course be taken for graduation from high school, up from one in 1998. In their study on the effects of financial education mandates, Gutter et al. (2009) found that simply having a standard was a key tipping point in increasing financial knowledge. Further, a more rigorous standard requiring courses and assessment had an even stronger impact. They suggest a minimum of having standards in place, with requiring courses and assessment as the ideal. These findings are important to remember as we discuss the importance of financial education and its role in economics curriculum.

While personal finance education mandates vary across the United States, there is a strong case that students need to be provided with sufficient opportunities to learn how to manage their personal finances wisely. The case is twofold:

1. Reliable research shows that students can benefit individually from personal finance education. Students are not receiving much instruction and have a low level of personal financial literacy, but significant improvements are possible.
2. In addition to the individual benefits to students, there are good reasons to believe the entire financial system can be more efficient when it is populated with financially educated individuals.

The argument for individual benefits from personal finance education starts with teen spending. While teen spending was down about 14 percent between spring of 2008 and spring of 2009, teens still spend an average of $125 billion a year (Zmuda, 2009). However, as teens and young adults continue to spend hundreds of billions of dollars a year, research has found that their personal financial literacy is very low.

Low financial literacy is a serious problem, especially for young adults entering college, the armed forces, or the work force who have never been directly or solely responsible for their own financial well-being in the past. Biannual studies by the Jump$tart Coalition consistently show low levels of financial knowledge among high school students. In 1997, students received an average score of 57 percent on financial questions related to taxes, retirement, insurance, credit use, inflation, and budgeting (Jump$tart, 1997). According to Jump$tart's 2004 study, these scores decreased to 50 percent in 2002 before reversing the declining trend in 2004 with average scores reaching 52.3 percent. Still, 65.5 percent of students failed the exam in 2004 and only 6.1 percent received a score of C or better (Jump$tart, 2004). Not only is financial knowledge low among teens and young adults, but this low knowledge oftentimes translates into less than desirable financial behaviors. Sallie Mae (2009) reports that college students are carrying record high levels of credit card debt. Between 2004 and 2008, the median credit card debt per student rose from $946 to $1,645, while the mean debt per student was $3,173. In addition, the younger population under the age of 25 continues to be one of the largest growing groups filing into bankruptcy by debtors, with numbers of bankruptcies in this group increasing by 51 percent from 1991 to 1999 (United States General Accounting Office, 2001).

While low financial knowledge and poor financial behaviors are cause for concern, incorporating personal finance education into high school economics courses is a possible solution. Several earlier studies (Langrehr, 1979; Langrehr and Mason, 1978; Peterson, 1992) found that students' knowledge improved significantly in the subject area studied after taking a specific course in economics or consumer education. These results have also been supported by more recent studies. Danes and Haberman (2004) found that students reported significant improvements in their financial knowledge immediately after studying the High School Financial Planning Program (HSFPP) offered by the National Endowment for Financial Education in the 2003–2004 school year. Similarly, Danes et al. (1999) found that immediately after studying the HSFPP curriculum, almost half of the students increased their knowledge regarding the cost of credit, auto insurance, and investments, with the highest knowledge gains seen in the area of credit cost. This increase in knowledge was not short-lived either. At a three-month follow-up, students still showed statistically significant increases on all questions except the one about their investment knowledge.

Increases in financial knowledge are exciting, but the main goal of personal finance education continues to be improving actual financial behaviors of students. In congruence with the increase in financial knowledge, Danes et al. (1999) found that immediately after studying the HSFPP curriculum, about 40 percent of the students increased positive financial behaviors including writing goals to manage their money, saving money for their needs and wants, and tracking their expenses. Again, at a three-month follow-up, approximately 60 percent of the students indicated that they had changed their spending patterns to spend more wisely and only include things that they really need. In addition, 60 percent of students had changed their savings patterns, with 80 percent of those students saving for what they really need or want and 20 percent saving every time they get money. Varcoe et al. (2005) found that saving behavior significantly increased after participating in the *Money Talks* curriculum. Participants also indicated that their shopping behavior had improved because they were more likely to compare prices and wait until items were on sale. Lyons (2008) also found that students who were currently taking, or who had taken, a formal course in personal finance were significantly less likely to engage in risky financial behaviors.

From all of this information, we see three things: (1) many students across the United States are receiving minimal to no personal finance education in their schools; (2) many students have low financial literacy relating to financial knowledge and financial behaviors;

and (3) financial education has been found to have a positive relationship on both financial knowledge and financial behaviors. It seems appropriate, then, that personal finance education be integrated into the high school curriculum to provide students with the opportunity of becoming informed consumers so that they can engage in positive financial behaviors.

Even beyond the individual benefits, however, there is reason to believe there may be benefits to the entire system from personal finance education. Improving consumer financial capability through personal finance education may actually lead to greater efficiency in the financial marketplace. Recent research has focused on the possible origins of volatility in asset markets. That is, why do stock and bond markets swing up and down so strongly? Why, for example, did stock indexes fall to less than half of their pre-crisis value by March 9, 2009 (Holt, 2009)?

In an intriguing class of models, the markets are populated not only by well informed traders but also by "noise traders." The noise traders do not study the market and do not commit to long-term strategies. Instead, they buy when they think others are buying and sell when they think others are selling. Noise traders are said to follow "positive feedback strategies," buying when prices go up and selling when prices go down (De Long et al., 1990). The presence of noise traders makes markets more volatile. In fact, as De Long et al. (1990) showed, noise traders can even cause rational traders to pursue more speculative strategies, further adding to volatility.

Personal finance education, by stressing the importance of long-term planning and sensible investment strategies, can over time reduce the number of noise traders. Since noise trading can infect any asset market, from stocks and bonds to real estate, the potential for benefit is large.

Consider one additional example from the recent economic crisis, specifically the sub-prime mortgage market. While under the Truth in Lending Act lenders would have provided full disclosure of mortgage terms and details to borrowers (United States, 2007), there is concern that consumers may not have fully understood the implications of a change in interest rates on their mortgage payments (Powell and Roberts, 2009). Further, since only 63.9 percent of consumers are using spending plans (Consumer Action, 2005), many may not have understood how such changes would actually impact their budgets. In addition, those without emergency funds or plans may have had difficulty maintaining their mortgage payments with reduced or loss of income in some instances, even in the short run. The next sections will discuss the connection between personal finance and economics, as well as the place of personal finance education in the economics classroom.

Connecting Personal Finance to Economics

We have seen the importance of financial education, but some may ask why personal finance should be taught in the economics classroom. The main justification is that the principles of personal financial education are grounded in economic theory. Indeed economics helps to explain savings, consumption, investing, and insurance behaviors. In this way, the same principles that guide microeconomics also guide personal financial management. What better way to connect economics to reality than to teach students how to relate these theories to their own lives? And what better time than when markets and financial institutions are changing rapidly?

Personal financial management is often seen from the perspective of Family Resource Management or Family Economics. A critical aspect of economic theory is that consumers will make rational decisions. However, in order to make rational decisions, consumers must have the relevant information about a decision and have a process in place to make such decisions. Another aspect of economic theory, specifically the life-cycle hypothesis, is that individuals seek to smooth consumption over their lifetimes. We will further examine the connection between personal finance and economics by looking at several important areas of personal finance related to rational decision-making and other important economic concepts.

Savings is often conceptualized as trading current consumption for future consumption. Modigliani and Brumberg's (1954, 1980) life-cycle hypothesis provides a framework for this decision, but again, assumes that individuals will behave rationally. The problem here is that individuals do not always behave rationally when it comes to personal finance. Oftentimes, instead of rationally planning to save, individuals save only what is left over (if there is anything left over) at the end of the month. Still, many families are trying to maximize lifetime satisfaction through allocation of finite resources over time. As Gutter et al. (2008) discuss, economic theory provides a base understanding of personal finance that can be enhanced with both psychological and sociological considerations.

Consumption behavior as a whole is often explored through neo-classical demand theory. The basic principle here is that rational people seek to get the most utility that they can out of their money. For consumers, this would indicate the need to plan for expenses through budgeting, shop around for the best prices, invest wisely, save for emergencies, and plan for retirement, among other things. For example, E. Scott Maynes' (1978) work on search cost suggests that rational consumers should search for information on prices, services, and so forth for as long as the expected gain from the search exceeds its expected cost. It is important to remember, however, that expected gains and costs are not purely economical but include things such as opportunity cost and willingness to take financial risks.

This is an example of how application of economic theory can be brought into the classroom through personal finance education. Economic theory starts out assuming that people make rational decisions and that they are rationally acquiring the information they need to make these decisions. However, if people make financial decisions under conditions of imperfect information, it is possible to improve the information set through financial education so that people can have greater lifetime wealth. For example, educational topics such as the effects of compound interest will provide students with the information necessary to understand that saving a small amount regularly can lead to a more prosperous retirement. A related issue is one of information asymmetry, where service providers and firms have more information than consumers or simply that consumers lack the knowledge to interpret the information. For example, the terms of an Adjustable Rate Mortgage are clearly disclosed, yet some will not fully grasp the impact of such a choice. In the mortgage crisis of 2007–2009, some consumers simply did not understand the risks they were taking with sub-prime loans (Powell and Roberts, 2009).

Investment behaviors and money management strategies are certainly guided by economics. Understanding the market economy and basic concepts such as time value of money and supply and demand are essential to proper investment management. For example, the demand for risky assets is affected by the risk aversion of the individual. This concept is conceptualized by Arrow (1971) and Pratt (1964). Further, Friend and Blume (1975) established a formal relationship between relative risk aversion and the portfolio allocation to risky assets.

Another area in which personal finance can be connected to economics is in the area of insurance behavior. Insurance behavior is a function of decision-making under uncertainty, meaning that the probability of each possible outcome occurring is unknown (Vaughan and Vaughan, 2008). Modern decision theory suggests that, in congruence with Pascal's wager, when the probability of a loss cannot be determined, one should choose the option that provides the lowest potential for loss. This idea, called the minimax (a.k.a. minimize maximum regret) strategy, is the basis for insurance and should be applied when the maximum cost associated with a certain outcome is not acceptable to the individual (Vaughan and Vaughan, 2008). By taking this strategy into account, students will be better able to make rational financial decisions regarding their own insurance.

This section has demonstrated the connection between personal finance and economics and has shown that the two can be integrated into the same classroom setting. However, what is the best way to achieve such integration? The next section discusses strategies and resources for instructors who want to incorporate personal finance into their economics class.

Teaching Strategies and Resources

The first step for an instructor is to determine whether the goal is to simply teach concepts or to have an experience at higher levels of cognition such as synthesis, application, and evaluation. Is the course about knowledge or changing behavior itself? Depending on the answers to these questions, there are different resources and strategies for instructors to consider.

We will focus on four basic approaches: standard classroom, case studies, simulations, and service learning.

Standard Classroom

The standard classroom approach would be the least intense approach for students. This approach would be most appropriate for classes in which the main goal is to teach knowledge and concepts. This would include standard procedures such as PowerPoint lectures and guided discussion with students taking notes. The standard classroom approach can also be combined with each of the other three approaches in order to create a more dynamic learning experience. Two examples of broad curriculum include HSFPP and FDIC *Money Smart*. In addition there are many specific programs for focused topics such as *Understanding Taxes* from the IRS (2010). There are also programs related to entrepreneurship from organizations like Junior Achievement. One can use the Jump$tart Coalition's Clearinghouse (2010) to search for different programs appropriate for youth.

The Academy of Financial Services and Certified Financial Planner Board of Standards, Inc. have a joint model financial planning curriculum (2010) that may also be helpful. At either website there are examples of syllabi for various financial planning settings. The following strategies can be used to build on the basic information covered during lectures and discussions.

Case Studies

The case study approach allows students to look at a hypothetical financial case for an individual and family, analyze it, and make suggestions to improve the financial situation. Cases can be broad and encompass a full financial profile of the individual or family, or they can be narrower to deal with specific areas such as saving, budgeting, investing, or purchasing insurance. This approach allows students to evaluate a financial situation, synthesize what they have learned, and apply what they have learned to improve that situation. One example of case study books is *Real Life Financial Planning with Case Studies* (Bransom, 2006). In addition, some instructors prefer students to create their own case study following certain criteria or to work with a real family. These case studies are probably only useful for advanced classes.

Simulations

A simulation approach to learning about personal finance can also be very effective. In this approach, students are able to imitate real-life situations and work through real-life problems in the classroom setting. Simulations can help students not only to apply concepts, but also to do so in a setting that mimics actual markets where they will participate in the future. According to Barbara O'Neill (2008, p. 1) "keys to a successful simulation experience are easy to replicate materials, realistic scenarios, clear instructions for participants, and a thorough debriefing where students discuss their experiences and what they learned." Simulations can allow students to practice basic skills such as check-writing and creating a budget, but they can also allow students to practice more advanced skills such as choosing investments. O'Neill (2008) provides a list and description of a number of current interactive group simulations that are available for use.

Some examples of programs like this include a Poverty Simulation, Reality Store, and other budgeting simulations. These programs can be used to help students make resource allocation decisions. Students must make it through a simulated month making decisions about what to spend money on. They typically have families to feed, bills to pay, and other decisions. Chance cards are a regular part of such simulations to see how students react to a change to their financial plan. It is important to have a reflection or debriefing activity so students can review their choices and discuss their logic with others.

Stock market simulations provide an excellent way to teach students about investment markets, transaction basics, selecting investments, and investment principles. They allow for ongoing activity of a hypothetical account. Students make regular transactions buying and selling securities. Many instructors allow for use of mutual funds, too, as these are common vehicles many will encounter through employer-provided plans. While there are many stock market simulations for classroom use, the Stock Market Game™ (SIMFA, 2010) is popular among many teachers. In times of high market volatility, there are lessons both for the students who win and for the students who lose.

Service Learning

Service learning is an approach that combines classroom curriculum with meaningful community service. This approach allows students to not only apply what they have learned, but to help others in the process. Service learning opportunities could include such things as volunteering at a local VITA tax preparation site, peer-mentoring younger children in how to budget and save, running a credit union in the school, or any other of a variety of meaningful opportunities that are available.

Conclusion

Students, as consumers, are expected to behave rationally as a function of economic theory but often have imperfect information upon which to make financial decisions. Market efficiency depends on an informed consumer to make prudent decisions. Since this is the case, personal financial education has an important void to fill in order to provide students with the accurate information they need to make rational decisions. As financially educated students graduate and go out into the community, their better choices can also improve the stability of the overall system. As has been established in this chapter, the economics classroom is an ideal location for the integration of personal financial education at the high school level. Depending on the level of learning desired, personal financial education can be integrated in several ways. Basic knowledge can be presented through the means of lecture materials in the standard classroom setting. More advanced synthesis and application can be reached through using techniques such as case studies, simulations, and service learning opportunities.

References

Academy of Financial Services and Certified Financial Planner Board of Standards, Inc. (2010). *Model financial planning curriculum.* Retrieved from: www.academyfinancial.org/afscfp.html.

Arrow, K.J. (1971). The theory of risk aversion. In *Essays in the theory of risk bearing.* Chicago: Markham Publishing Co.

Bransom, T.D. (2006). *Real life financial planning with case studies.* United States: Aspatore, Inc.

Consumer Action. (2005). *National MoneyWi$e survey shows Americans are not financially fit* (press release, September 6, 2005). Retrieved from: www.consumer- action.org/press/articles/national_moneywie_survey_shows_americans_are_not_financially_fit.

Council on Economic Education (CEE). (2009). *Survey of the States: Economic, personal finance and entrepreneurship education in our nation's schools in 2009.* New York: Council on Economic Education. Retrieved from: www.councilforeconed.org/about/survey2009.

Danes, S.M. and Haberman, H. (2004). *2003–2004 evaluation of the NEFE HSFPP.* Retrieved December 10, 2004, from: www.nefe.org/hsfpppor-tal/includes/main/home.asp?page=4000#evaluation2.

Danes, S.M., Huddleston-Casas, C.A., and Boyce, L. (1999). Financial planning curriculum for teens: Impact evaluation. *Financial Counseling and Planning, 10*(1), 25–37.

De Long, J.B., Shleifer, A., Summers, L.H., and Waldmann, R.J. (1990). Positive feedback investment strategies and destabilizing rational speculation. *The Journal of Finance, 45*(2), 379–395.

Friend, I. and Blume, M. (1975). The demand for risky assets. *The American Economic Review, 65*(5), 900–922.

Gutter, M.S., Copur, Z., and Garrison, S.T. (2009, July). *Are high school financial education policy differences related to differences in college student financial behaviors?* Paper presented at the annual meeting of the American Council on Consumer Interests, Milwaukee, WI.

Gutter, M.S., Hayhoe, C.R., and DeVaney, S. (2008). Economical and psychological determinants of savings behavior: A conceptual model. *Consumer Interests Annual, 54*, 197–198.

Holt, J. (2009). A summary of the primary causes of the housing bubble and the resulting credit crisis: A non-technical paper. *The Journal of Business Inquiry, 8*(1), 120–129.

Jump$tart Coalition. (1997). *High school seniors lack financial smarts shows survey.* American Savings Education Council News Release.

Jump$tart Coalition. (2004). *Making the case for financial literacy.* American Savings Education Council News Release.

Jump$tart Coalition. (2010). *Jump$tart coalition clearinghouse.* Retrieved from: www.jumpstart.org/search.cfm.

Langrehr, F.W. (1979). Consumer education: Does it change students' competencies and attitudes? *Journal of Consumer Affairs, 13*(1), 14–53.

Langrehr, F.W. and Mason, J.B. (1978). The influence of formal instruction in consumer education academic units on attitudes toward the marketplace: A case study of Illinois students. *Journal of Economic Education, 9*, 133–134.

Lyons, A.C. (2008). Risky credit card behavior of college students. In J.J. Xiao (Ed.), *Handbook of consumer finance research* (pp. 185–208). New York: Springer.

Maynes, E.S. (1978). Attitudes, behaviors, and economics. In J.M. Yinger and S.J. Cutler (Eds.), *Major social issues: A multidisciplinary approach* (pp. 390–411). New York: Free Press.

Modigliani, F. and Brumberg, R. (1954). Utility analysis and the consumption function: An interpretation of cross-section data. In K.K. Kurihara

(Ed.), *Post-Keynesian economics* (pp. 388–436). New Brunswick: Rutgers University Press.

Modigliani, F. and Brumberg, R. (1980). Utility analysis and aggregate consumption functions: An attempt at integration. In A. Abel (Ed.), *The collected papers of Franco Modigliani* (pp. 128–197). Cambridge, MA: MIT Press.

O'Neill, B. (2008). Financial simulations for young adults: Making the "real world" real. *Journal of Extension* [On-line], *46*(6), Article 6TOT4. Retrieved from: www.joe.org/joe/2008december/pdf/JOE_v46_6tot4. pdf.

Peterson, N.A. (1992). The high school economics course and its impact on economic knowledge. *Journal of Economic Education, 23*(1), 5–16.

Powell, M. and Roberts, J. (2009). Minorities affected most as New York foreclosures rise. *New York Times*, A1. May 15, 2009.

Pratt, K.J. (1964). Risk aversion in the small and large. *Econometrica, 32*(1–2), 122–136.

Sallie Mae. (2009). How undergraduate students use credit cards. *Sallie Mae's National Study of Usage Rates and Trends 2009.*

Securities Industry and Financial Markets Association (SIMFA) Foundation. (2010). *The Stock Market game.* Retrieved from: http://stockmarketgame. org.

United States. (2007). *Providing for consideration of the bill (H.R. 3915) to amend the Truth in Lending Act to reform consumer mortgage practices and provide accountability for such practices, to establish licensing and registration requirements for residential mortgage originators, to provide certain minimum standards for consumer mortgage loans, and for other purposes: Report (to accompany H. Res. 825).* Washington, D.C.: U.S. G.P.O.

United States General Accounting Office. (2001). *Consumer finance: College students and credit cards (GAO#01–773).* Washington, DC: Author.

U.S. Internal Revenue Service. (2010). Understanding taxes. Retrieved from: www.irs.gov/app/understandingTaxes/index.jsp.

VanDerhei, J. (2009). The impact of the recent financial crisis on 401(k) account balances. *Pension Benefits, 18*(5), 10–11.

Varcoe, K.P., Allen, M., Devitto, Z., and Go, C. (2005). Using a financial education curriculum for teens. *The Journal of the Association for Financial Counseling and Planning Education, 16*, 63–71.

Vaughan, E.J. and Vaughan, T. (2008). *Fundamentals of risk and insurance* (10th ed.). Hoboken, NJ: John Wiley & Sons.

Zmuda, N. (2009). Teens, too, are tightening budgets. *Advertising Age, 80*(15). Retrieved from: http://adage.com/article?article_id=136253.

9

ENTREPRENEURSHIP EDUCATION, WHEN AND WHERE IT COUNTS
The American Dream Youthpreneurship Program

Barbara Flowers

Entrepreneurship Education in High School

Although there have always been good reasons to teach entrepreneurship in high school, those reasons have multiplied with recent structural changes in the economy. Few students graduating today can count on steady employment at a single firm to make a career; instead, rapid turnover is more likely (Bureau of Labor Statistics, 2008). Bright students with a desire to succeed may find entrepreneurship more attractive than working for someone else. But how can they get started? This chapter sets forth principles of high school entrepreneurship education based on experience with the American Dream Youthpreneurship Program in St. Louis.

Principle 1: The Teenage Years Can Be the Ideal Time for an Entrepreneurial Venture

Earning an income by washing cars, cutting grass, making jewelry, or babysitting is a practical alternative for students with irregular schedules due to their increased schoolwork, club activities, and sports. Self-employment is a feasible option when traditional summer and part-time jobs are less available to teenagers (*ABC News*, 2009).

Operating a grass-cutting service certainly requires little study, and yet it can prompt a desire to seek other, more complex, entrepreneurial ventures. High school educators can take advantage of teenage enthusiasm for entrepreneurship as a teaching opportunity. However,

135

comprehensive entrepreneurship education involves an array of concepts, from the knowledge an individual must have (or quickly acquire) to start and have control of a successful business to an understanding of the shocks that can affect a business and how they may be foreseen and managed. How can entrepreneurship education be introduced in the high school curriculum? This chapter describes one method.

There are many entrepreneurship programs in high school education, and each has value. Approaches range from operating a classroom business or an after-school business club, to operating an arbitrage operation, to individual students striking out on their own. While there are a variety of approaches, helping students recognize and take advantage of opportunities on their own is at the heart of the entrepreneurial experience.

Principle 2: Classroom Businesses Have Their Shortcomings for Teaching Entrepreneurial Values

The classroom business is a fine exercise in small business development but is it entrepreneurial? Generally, classroom businesses involve having student producers. Common products are cookies, calendars, and greeting cards. Students take roles in sales, bookkeeping, marketing, management, and production. Each of these roles furthers their knowledge, but at least two essential components are missing: the origin of the idea and the element of risk. The ideas may have come from the teacher or they may have come from students but, ultimately, for most of the students involved, it is an exercise in democracy. Ideas are listed, and the class votes. At that point, it becomes a game of follow the leader. Students are directed and managed, much like they would be in any after-school job. Risk is non-existent. Students have no financial risk, they have no reputational risk, and, most of all, they are not even risking the rejection of their idea, because the idea was not theirs. Will the students gain much more entrepreneurial inspiration from the classroom exercise in baking and selling cookies than they would in frying and selling hamburgers? Without experiencing the element of risk when operating a small business, will they be able to discern the risk when assessing actual business opportunities in their futures? There are numerous pitfalls to entrepreneurship, with the misunderstanding of risk at the top of the list (National Consumer League, 2010).

The arbitrage approach involves buying products at a low price to sell in a different market at a higher price. In one setting this might be called entrepreneurship education and in another setting it is called a fund-raiser. Once again, as a classroom business, it has its value in teaching some of the approaches to operating a small business. However, it lacks the opportunity-recognition component that is essential to the entrepreneurial venture. In other arbitrage approaches, students are challenged as individuals to see how successful they can be in purchasing products for resale to other students. For example, a student may purchase bulk no. 2 pencils and sell them during lunch periods. Some of these programs provide the students with the money to buy a product to sell. Opportunity recognition is limited to the products in their price range available at the store. The risk is low because the money could not have been used by the student for any other purpose.

Even with their drawbacks, it is easy to understand why these types of entrepreneurship programs are attractive. Certain essential concepts are conveyed, such as the importance of keeping accurate records or of market identification. For classes containing entrepreneurship as a "unit," these programs fit the time frame. Finally, students can experience success in these programs. A cookie sale can raise a nice profit, and it feels good to have out-earned the other students in the class by choosing to sell no. 2 pencils.

A comprehensive program in entrepreneurship involves learning and practice. It is not enough to introduce the promises of entrepreneurship without providing solid information on a broad array of concepts. It may seem that teaching entrepreneurship would be a challenge because most teachers have no experience in recognizing an opportunity and building it into a profitable business. However, the lessons that must be learned are well within the teacher's scope of knowledge and teaching ability.

Principle 3: Opportunity Recognition Is a Vital Concept to Teach

Most programs begin with an analysis of general entrepreneurial traits. Students study biographical information on entrepreneurs looking for examples of ambition, tenacity, organization, risk-taking, optimism, and so on. Entrepreneurs may share these traits, but in reality, there is no particular personality type, and the traits attributed to the entrepreneur can just as easily be observed in politicians, researchers, high-level managers, and teachers. The common thread among entrepreneurs is their ability to spot an opportunity and their willingness to act on it, even in difficult times. In fact, Brad Sugars (2009) suggests that a recession may be the best time to start a new business. Some entrepreneurs are motivated by inspiration, and some are motivated by desperation.

So, an entrepreneurship education program should begin with an examination not of the entrepreneur and his product, but of the path the entrepreneur took toward discovery. What prompted the idea? The answer is unique to every entrepreneur, but there are some common paths, whether they are through invention, innovation, education, or expertise developed through experience. Perhaps the trait most common is passion for the idea. This is not necessarily passion for the product, but the belief that he or she can provide the product better than anyone else. The first step, therefore, in entrepreneurship education is opportunity recognition.

Entrepreneurs recognize the opportunity to offer value. Whether it is a new method of broadcasting your news of the day (Facebook) to finding a way to wrap yourself in a blanket while holding your coffee (Snuggie), entrepreneurs seek ways to make people's activities more fun, better organized, less expensive, and more efficient.

High school students seem adept at opportunity recognition. Perhaps it is the impatience of youth, but, as observed in the program to be described in this chapter, as well as in the many other entrepreneurship programs available to teachers, teens find a great deal of shortcomings in the products they consume and are eager to promote their improvements.

Principle 4: ("Have An Idea! Now What?") Business Plans Are an Excellent Organizing Tool That Can Save Teenage Entrepreneurs from Common Mistakes

After students have a product in mind, the real work begins. Let the business plan be your guide. Many entrepreneurs will admit that they have never developed a formal business plan. While that may be true, it is essential in entrepreneurship education for its organizational value. Using a comprehensive business plan template ensures that most details of business development will be considered.

During annual entrepreneurship competitions at the University of Missouri–St. Louis, it was obvious which students had seriously considered all aspects of a business plan and which had not. The most often overlooked details of the business were in the accounting areas. Perhaps it's just human nature to underestimate expenses (just think about your last vacation), but the students failed to include cost items that would have become evident in their research had they followed a business plan template.

The teenage entrepreneurs typically underestimated explicit costs (and overestimated revenue). A well developed business plan would have made students aware of the explicit costs, and, indirectly, implicit costs—those costs associated with the resources owned by the entrepreneur. For example, the jewelry makers might record the costs of beads, but disregard the cost of the fishing line they found in the tackle box in the garage. The muffin baker might record the costs of the ingredients, but overlook that there are costs associated with the muffin tins and the stove. A business plan would allow the jewelry maker to recognize that eventually she will come to the end of the fishing line and will have the expense of purchasing it.

The most often overlooked cost was the students' labor. They recognized that the return to entrepreneurship is profit. However, when they subtracted their expenses from their revenue, and found themselves to be profitable, they seemed oblivious to the opportunity cost of spending their time creating their product. One young woman reported that the profit from the production of a personalized tote bag was $10. When asked how many hours it took to create the tote bag, she responded that she really didn't know but estimated it took five hours. The judge asked her if she would be willing to work after school for $2 an hour. Her answer was a resounding "No." Of course, many businesses start out at a loss with the entrepreneur expecting it to become profitable as people become more familiar with the product. However, it was clear in her later explanation that she didn't understand the opportunity cost of her labor. A comprehensive business plan template accounts for every explicit cost of production, and with a simple examination of the source of each resource, will also reveal the implicit costs associated with production.

The business plan also helps students determine their market, and thus, their marketing strategy. Communication has changed over the years of this program's operation. In recent years, students referred to a marketing strategy that involved web pages and social network systems. In the past, the strategies involved fliers and word-of-mouth. Students often concentrated more on the form of communication rather than the make-up of their customer base. Regardless of the method of communication, the business plan helps students clarify their market. They recognize that their target market determines the communication method and they avoid simply engaging in a communication strategy while hoping it reaches their target market. In a time when potential customers were flush with cash, student entrepreneurs might have gotten away with a less than stellar communication strategy. Today, effectiveness of communication is vital.

Principle 5: Personal Finance and Credit Education Are Necessary for
Entrepreneurs to Be Able to Fund Their Start-ups

Students are under the misconception that the money to start a business is easily obtained through a bank, from investors, or perhaps even a government grant. Many of them are unaware of the "credit crunch" and banks' wariness about lending (Tozzi, 2008). The real story is that entrepreneurs must invest their own money in their venture. If the entrepreneur has so little confidence in the idea that he is unwilling to invest, why should anyone else take this leap of faith? So, among all the lessons of entrepreneurship, personal finance must be at the forefront. With an eye toward beginning a business in the future, students must recognize that they must commit their savings or property, and they must have a credit rating sufficiently high to earn them the trust of a bank and suppliers.

A strategy for saving is important, but the saving can't happen without an income. Of course, the income can be generated through a part-time job, but it can also be generated through an entrepreneurial venture, and that venture can provide valuable experience for a larger venture in the future. In either case, students must learn how to handle their income, with an emphasis on their spending/saving ratio and taxes. An examination of payroll taxes in itself is a lesson in entrepreneurship. For example, the student will be subject to a 7.65 percent Social Security tax, but will see that the employer is responsible for another 7.65 percent. The process of preparing paychecks is another lesson that shouldn't be overlooked. As students study payroll deductions, they will recognize the complexity in determining how much must be withheld from the employee and how that is the responsibility of the business owner.

Education in the wise use of credit is essential. As mentioned earlier, a fledgling business has no credit history, so the ability to gain credit depends on the creditworthiness of the entrepreneur. The focus is often on the entrepreneur's ability to get a bank loan for her start-up. However, the entrepreneur relies on credit for capital investment as the business grows and for the timely delivery of components and supplies. There are many quality personal finance lessons and programs to help students understand credit. Most important, students must establish credit and maintain a strong credit rating. To do this, they can establish a checking account and avoid overdrafts. They can buy their own car insurance or cell phone contract and pay on time.

Principle 6: Economic Education Is Essential to Entrepreneurship Education

The economy poses risks to entrepreneurs that are beyond their immediate control. If product components are not delivered on time because an employee failed to order on time, the entrepreneur can address the problem and be assured that it is corrected. If the component is not delivered because the supplier suddenly goes out of business, the entrepreneur faces a problem that is beyond her control.

As the financial market meltdown and recession of 2008–2009 illustrated, an understanding of macroeconomic fluctuations is essential to the entrepreneur's survival. Students must learn basic macroeconomic concepts related to business cycles. For example, what is likely to happen to the demand for the product during periods of high unemployment? The demand for many goods and services will decrease as people's incomes decrease, in the case of a normal good. However, the demand for some goods actually increases as people's income decrease. These are inferior goods.

Furthermore, the demand for resources is derived from the demand for the good or service the resource is used to produce. So, entrepreneurs offering either intermediate goods or resources may find the decline in the demand for their goods delayed but will likely find that they have not escaped the economic downturn, unless the good produced with the resource is an inferior good. In that case, the demand for the intermediate good or resource would likely increase. This is an insight that is missed in general entrepreneurship education materials that do not include economic education.

If the entrepreneur is savvy and the downturn is not too deep or too lengthy, he can look forward to an economic upswing. This is a time of sales and profits (assuming he sells a normal good). However, even expansions can be accompanied by unpleasant economic phenomena.

In the late 1990s, the expansion created very low rates of unemployment. In some areas, the unemployment rate was so low that entrepreneurs could not find enough workers and, in some cases, could not keep the workers they had as other employers bid up wages to attract workers to their enterprises. Economic expansion can also lead to inflation as people's incomes increase, leading to an increase in demand for goods and services. Inflation can be tough on the entrepreneur who must make difficult decisions as to whether to raise prices and wages. Raising prices will reduce the amount of product they will sell, and perhaps their total revenue. Maintaining current wages may cause them to lose employees as other firms attract workers by offering higher wages.

Following the 2008–2009 financial market meltdown, the problems for entrepreneurs were reversed. Employees were easy to find and materials costs were under control. The main problem was a lack of demand for final output, putting a premium on having gauged the market correctly to offer the right products at the right time.

Students will likely only get this education through a course in economics. It is easy to see how a misunderstanding of business cycles could lead to the entrepreneurial venture's demise.

The "How To": How the American Dream Youthpreneurship Program Works

Although the challenges of entrepreneurship education may seem daunting, the American Dream Youthpreneurship Program provides a working model and an illustration of what is possible. The program consists of three components: a credit course, Teaching Entrepreneurship; the Entrepreneurship Institute; and the Entrepreneurship Competition.

The credit course consists of five full days of study during the summer, followed by three classes during the fall semester. The curriculum includes strategies for teaching opportunity recognition, business plan development, personal finance awareness, and the introduction of basic microeconomic and macroeconomic concepts. It would be naive to attempt to teach all concepts in depth. The goal of the class is to introduce the concepts and identify them as essential knowledge for successful business operation.

The teachers in the class are required to interview an entrepreneur, develop a modified business plan based on their own business idea, design their own plan for implementing entrepreneurship in their classes, correlate their plan with their state educational standards, develop an assessment tool, and create a journal of their experience in teaching their plan.

The interview helps to solidify the instructor's contention that an understanding of personal finance and economic concepts is essential. It also serves the purpose of demonstrating that entrepreneurs are ordinary people who take the extraordinary step of starting a business. For the instructor, it serves the purpose of bringing additional entrepreneurs into the program to serve as coaches, speakers, and judges.

The business plan development is an exercise in modeling what will be asked of the high school students. This assignment helps teachers recognize the organizational value of the plan. However, it has had the unanticipated benefit of actual business development. A few teachers have initiated their businesses as part-time operations.

The implementation plan is the most essential of the assignments because it places entrepreneurship education into the course curriculum. Teachers taking the Teaching Entrepreneurship course come from an assortment of disciplines. As expected, many come from business education; however, their courses may be limited to marketing, accounting, or office software. Others come from social studies, where entrepreneurship might be taught in conjunction with economics, civics, or personal finance. (One social studies teacher taught World History and incorporated the program as a unit on "Ancient Entrepreneurs.") Still others in the program come from vocational or art programs. Each implementation plan is, therefore, unique and must be carefully integrated. The thought and care that go into the plan virtually assure that it will be taught.

The correlation of the program with the state standards and the assessment tool are included to assist the teacher in justifying the course (or unit) to the administration. Each program is unique, so each will address different standards within business or social studies, but may also address standards in math and communication arts.

The journal is a common tool in graduate education classes. In this case, it provides a record of the effectiveness of the entrepreneurship education lessons and prompts changes to the implementation plan.

Teachers are drawn to entrepreneurship education for a variety of reasons. Most of them believe this line of education will eventually create entrepreneurs and all the benefits entrepreneurs bring to the economy. Vocational teachers who are involved in courses, such as culinary arts, cosmetology, and graphic design, are aware that careers in these areas often lead to a desire to establish one's own business. In the case of this program, some teachers appreciate the direct contact students have working with entrepreneurs during the Entrepreneurship Institute and the awards for students who are successful in the Entrepreneurship Competition.

The Institute

Teachers who have taken the Teaching Entrepreneurship course are invited to bring their students to the annual Entrepreneurship Institute. The Institute is a two-day seminar/workshop that allows students to work directly with entrepreneurs. Teachers must commit to bring the same students to both days of the institute to allow students the full effect of spending two entire days working with practitioners. During the first day of the institute, students break into groups of 25–40 to work with two entrepreneurs. It requires 10–12 entrepreneurs to accommodate the entire group. An additional 10–12 entrepreneurs are required for the second day.

Recruiting entrepreneurs is an annual challenge. First, they are difficult to reach—because they are entrepreneurs! The timing of the invitation is also a challenge. If the invitation is extended early, they will likely be available on the day requested. However, if something very important were to come up between their acceptance and the Institute, they would likely apologetically decline. Business issues can also take place on the day of the Institute, forcing entrepreneurs' last-minute cancellations. It is always important to have back-ups. Finally, the Institute runs from 8:30 a.m. until 1:30 p.m. This is a substantial time commitment for the entrepreneur, who is also asked to lead three distinct tasks with the students. It is often necessary to book different entrepreneurs for different shifts, which, of course, requires a larger number of entrepreneurs.

The mix of entrepreneurs is important for a diverse student population. Generally speaking, entrepreneurs with long-established businesses often have larger staffs and more availability. However, every effort should be made to recruit a number of younger entrepreneurs with whom high school students more readily identify. Diversity in gender and ethnicity is also important. Most important is diversity of businesses. A sample of entrepreneurs who have participated in this program include a custom car builder, the proprietor of a do-it-yourself stuffed bear company, an artist, a greeting card publisher, a home health care company, companies providing computer applications of all sorts, cabinet makers, restaurant owners, and companies providing various spices and sauces. It is also important to invite not-for-profit entrepreneurs. Students are often confused by the term "not-for-profit," equating it with "not-for-wages." Ultimately, the not-for-profit businesses have often been the most popular with students, their curiosity evident by the number of questions. In some cases, the not-for-profits have gained volunteers from the Institute.

Only the students of teachers who have taken the course and are currently teaching entrepreneurship may attend the Institute. Although this rule has certainly attracted teachers to the course, the reason for this limitation is that entrepreneurs want to speak to students who understand basic business concepts and vocabulary so that the class can immediately get into the fundamentals of business development. Students are asked to come to the institute with a business idea they can use in one of the break-out exercises.

In the first break-out session, students attempt to discover the entrepreneur's business by asking questions in the format of "What's My Line?" After students have guessed correctly or the business has been revealed, the entrepreneurs discuss their businesses. There is purposely little guidance for the entrepreneurs. If they ask what to discuss, it is suggested that they discuss their opportunity recognition, the barriers they faced, and a favorite success story.

The entrepreneurs are asked to come prepared with a problem for the second break-out session—The Problem Solvers. Each entrepreneur presents a problem that he or she has experienced or that might occur with the business. The class is broken into two groups to address each problem and then into smaller groups to allow more individual input. The small groups present their solutions on flip-chart paper and hang it on the wall. Each group then visits each of the other posters, commenting on the other solutions. The entrepreneurs have the final word as they move from poster to poster. This is usually the entrepreneurs' favorite session. They find the students' solutions to be thoughtful and, sometimes, helpful.

During the third, and last, session of the day, entrepreneurs begin with their "elevator talk," a two-minute description of their businesses, followed by a discussion of why certain entrepreneurs concentrate on aspects that others ignore. They discuss the difference between a talk to a potential customer vs. a talk to a potential investor. The goal is to help students separate the important information from the superfluous. The entrepreneurs move from student to student to help with development of clear descriptions of the students' businesses. Often, additional coaches from the Small Business Association (SBA), the Service Corp of Retired Executives (SCORE), and Small Business Development Centers (SBDCs) are invited to help with this session.

Three weeks later, students return to the Institute prepared with a three-minute description of their businesses. However, during the first session, students once again meet two entrepreneurs. The goal is to have each student have met a minimum of four entrepreneurs. During the second session, students present their business ideas to the entrepreneurs who provide suggestions on how the idea can be better developed. Students are also welcome to make suggestions to their peers.

The final session of the institute is an answer to the question, "Now what?" Students are introduced to the first steps in developing a business, that is, their own human capital development. The entrepreneur can choose to guide students in an examination of the education they will need to operate their businesses successfully or can help them recognize the steps they will have to take to fund a start-up, including an examination of their own personal financial habits.

The Competition

Regardless of students' prudent saving habits, for students who have an idea they would like to pursue now, there are few financial avenues. In some cases, students have a small savings to invest. In other cases, parents are interested in investing. In most cases, however, these financial sources are impractical. The Competition was initiated to help students with some level of funding.

Students must be nominated by their teachers. After nomination, students are offered an entrepreneur as a coach. Nominations are accepted beginning in January for the late spring Competition. There are three tracks to which students can apply. The academic track provides students with the opportunity to present their businesses and receive feedback from the judges, who, again, are local entrepreneurs and small business development specialists from the SBA,

SCORE, or SBDCs. Students may enter the seed-money track which is a Competition for start-up funds. They may also enter the scholarship track which provides them with either a $2,500 or $1,000 annual and renewable scholarship to the University of Missouri–St. Louis. Scholarships must be negotiated each year. The number and amount of seed-money prizes depends on the level of funding each year.

Students must submit a modified business plan in advance of the Competition. On the day of the Competition, students are expected to bring any props, samples, or advertising that will aid them in describing their business. Each student is interviewed rather than asked to present. The interview begins with a question from the modified business plan but can take any direction based on their student's answers. Only the judges may ask questions of the students. The decision to limit questions to judges was made after parents of the contestants were observed challenging students in competition with their children—lesson learned!

Students are judged on numerous criteria having to do with their ability to discuss their business knowledgeably, their business plan, and the viability of their business. The top seed-money prize is typically $500, so the student must demonstrate that the business could be viable if he or she were to win that amount.

Program Leadership

At various times in the year, the American Dream Youthpreneurship Program requires full-time program management. Teacher recruitment for the up-coming summer class and student nominations for the Competition takes place in the early spring, followed by the Competition in the late spring. Course preparation takes place during the summer, culminating in the five-day portion of the class in late July. Entrepreneur recruitment begins in September for the November Institute. Follow-up classes with the teachers and the Entrepreneurship Institute take place during the fall, followed quickly by grading. Before you know it, it's early spring and the cycle begins again.

An advisory board is essential. The teacher course developed and improved over the early years of the program. The components of the Institute were studied for their effectiveness and changed several times. The Competition was initiated several years after the course and the Institute to meet the teachers' requests for a funding outlet for their students. All changes and initiatives were the result of the participation, careful observations, and expertise of the advisory board. The board consists of entrepreneurs, high school teachers, a high school student, SCORE members, SBA members, and university professors. The board is not only vital in maintaining a quality program, it is also a source of speakers, a willing group of back-up entrepreneurs, an enthusiastic connection for the recruitment of additional entrepreneurs, and an eager group of judges.

Barriers to Entrepreneurship Programs

The most significant barrier is also the most mundane: funding. The same tough economic times that increase the usefulness of entrepreneurship education also reduce the resources potentially available. The program requires an instructor and program manager. The course offers either full- or half-tuition scholarships for teachers, depending on funding availability. In addition, teachers are provided with classroom materials sufficient to cover a one-semester class. The program covers some level of bus transportation and substitute teacher fees for the Institute, as well as lunch for the 250–300 students, 15–25 teachers, and 10–16 entrepreneurs. Competition participants, along with their teachers and families, as well as judges and other invited guests are offered breakfast. Typically, there is $1,200 to $1,600 available for seed-money prizes. In total, the program costs approximately $27,000. However, it is easy to see how the program could be offered at much less expense. For example, students could bring their lunches to the Institute, or the Competition breakfast could consist of coffee and doughnuts rather than bacon and eggs. Regardless of how expenses are reduced, it is still necessary to secure some source of funds. Several foundations exist that include entrepreneurship and small business education in their list of priorities. Local entrepreneurs often provide as much as $500 toward program expenses, particularly seed-money prizes.

There are limitations on the number of students that can be accommodated at the Institute, which necessitates the limitation of teacher numbers in the course. Teachers who have taken the course are forever included in the Institute invitation. Some teachers have changed assignments, retired, or moved to administration, so new teachers are recruited for the course each year, with a limit of ten. Teachers are often recruited through word-of-mouth; however, inquiries also result from the annual spring program newsletter and a website announcement. A waiting list is maintained from year to year.

Many teachers express an interest in including entrepreneurship education but find it difficult to imagine how and where to fit it with their existing curriculum. This program maintains a collection of implementation plans instituted by teachers who have successfully accomplished integration. For example, an office software instructor had students choose a business and taught Word operations using tables, business outlines, and letters that pertained to the students' businesses. She taught Excel having students develop cost and revenue estimates, and she taught PowerPoint by having students develop their business presentations. Of course, this required extra work on the part of the teacher. A simple grading template was out of the question. However, she reported greater interest on the part of her students and, in general, greater levels of mastery.

One of the most difficult to understand barriers (and one of the strongest arguments for teaching entrepreneurship) is disdain for entrepreneurs. The argument is that the entrepreneur is motivated by greed and will fudge, scheme, and cheat in his quest for a profit. Entrepreneurs, and business in general, are never as popular in times of economic uncertainty as they are in boom times.

The argument against the notion of the entrepreneur's unethical behavior toward customers is simple. How long will a business that fudges on quality or cheats customers exist? Competition will quickly dispose of such a business. To the contrary, it could be argued that entrepreneurs would necessarily place high on the ethics scale when dealing with their customers. Entrepreneurs are unlikely to shirk; their fortune depends on their quick response, as well as their customers' confidence and satisfaction. It is often suggested that one of the attractions of entrepreneurship is the opportunity to be your own boss. While it may be that there is no manager giving him orders, the entrepreneur can have hundreds of bosses, and if he's lucky, thousands. The customer is the entrepreneur's boss.

Finally, teachers wonder if it is worth providing entrepreneurship education when it is estimated that only 6 to 10 percent of us are entrepreneurial. While it is true that the majority of high school students will become employees of others, it is difficult to predict just who the budding entrepreneurs might be. During the Institute, entrepreneurs will often recount their younger years, including their past failures, the first notions of their businesses, and their educational history. While most of the entrepreneurs completed college, a surprising number indicated that they had a mediocre high school record. Some indicated that their efforts were directed toward working and earning money, but others reported a general impatience.

This program was developed in partnership with an urban school district and, initially, was limited to students from that district. Many of the students resided in neighborhoods that were suffering from a lack of services as small businesses moved or closed. There was no illusion that these young students would soon fill those storefronts with viable businesses. However, practice in the development of a small business, and, for a number of students, the actual experience of developing a small business, whether successful or not, allowed students to learn from mistakes as well as from the steps they took in the right direction.

One of the professors on the advisory board described the experience. Many people have great ideas for new or improved products or methods (how many have you had?), yet they never act on them. They see business start-up as the "blob," this mass of decisions that overwhelm you. In reality, an entrepreneurial venture is a series of decisions. A problem arises; the entrepreneur solves the problem and follows that path until the next problem arises. High school students who begin a small business discover this at an age when they have little to lose. Later, when the stakes are higher, they may have the confidence to start a business, knowing that they do not have to have all of the answers to take that first step.

One of the entrepreneurs presenting at the Institute placed a transparency on the projector, displaying two rows totaling 12 business cards. Each card was his, and each displayed a different business. He explained that one of those cards identified his current business, one that he had operated for about five years at the time. The other cards were businesses that he had either sold or closed. He had closed most of them. His point was that each taught him something that he took to the next business. Each failure was a learning experience.

So, does an entrepreneurship program have something to offer those who will never develop a business? Yes! The exercise in small business development provides the benefits listed earlier in this chapter. However, by studying entrepreneurship, students can better understand the entrepreneur's motives. They learn that profitable businesses generate more jobs and that working for a profitable business can generate more opportunities, higher wage levels, more generous benefits, and greater job security. This fosters a better understanding of management decisions and, perhaps better communication and cooperation.

References

ABC News. (2009). *Summer job search proves tough for teens.* May 24, 2009. Retrieved from: http://abcnews.go.com/GMA/JobClub/story?id=7667589&page=1.

Bureau of Labor Statistics. (2008). *Employee tenure in 2008.* September 26, 2008. Retrieved from: www.bls.gov/news.release/tenure.nr0.htm.

National Consumer League. (2010). *Work-at-home scams.* Retrieved from: www.fraud.org/tips/internet/workathome.htm.

Sugars, B. (2009). *Top 10 reasons to start a business in a recession.* February 25, 2009. Retrieved from: www.entrepreneur.com/startingabusiness/startup-basics/startupbasicscolumnistbradsugars/article200342.html.

Tozzi, J. (2008). The credit crunch and small business. September 26, 2008. *Business Week.* Retrieved from: www.businessweek.com/smallbiz/content/sep2008/sb20080925_579510.htm.

10

ECONOMICS IN HISTORY
What Every High School Student and Teacher Needs to Know

Lucien Ellington

Historians work in a discipline with few inherent concepts and are obliged to draw upon many fields in recreating the past. In studying history, students need knowledge of the chronology of key events, their geographical settings, and the formation of political institutions and legal systems. Also, it is imperative in history classes that students comprehend how basic principles of economics have affected both individuals and societies in the past as well as the present. This understanding is invaluable in assisting young people to use economic analysis as a tool for rationally comprehending human action and, because of the extensive relationship between policy decisions and the economy, to become effective citizens.

Many young people see no relationship between the study of the past and understanding the present. The integration of economic concepts and analysis into historical studies is a superb pedagogical antidote to this problem. Basic economic literacy enables students to draw valid connections between past and present. Although every historical and contemporary event is unique in one sense, since antiquity people have more often than not responded predictably to economic incentives and disincentives, tax rates, economic freedom or the lack thereof, and fluctuating currency values.

For various reasons, authors of most school history texts, state and national standards, and curriculum materials seem seldom to incorporate systematic explanations of economic concepts or economic analysis in their work. Examples of this problem abound ranging from state standards that include Adam Smith and John Locke but draw no connections between their economic thought and contemporary economic institutions and issues, to world history text treatment of the British Industrial Revolution as a virtual crime against humanity.

One goal of this chapter is the integration of economic under-standing into history classrooms through utilization of five economics-based case studies of widely studied societies and events usually included in history curricula: Ancient Greece and Rome, Imperial China, Colonial British America, the British Industrial Revolution, and the U.S. Depression of the 1930s. A sixth case study is also included that is intended to facilitate teacher and student comprehension of current economic problems through identifying lessons that can be learned from comparisons of the economic pol-icies of the Great Depression with the Great Recession of 2007–2010. A table containing annotated descriptions of economic history pedagogical resources is also included in the chapter.

The Greco-Roman World and Economics: Athens

> As for poverty, no one need be ashamed to admit it: the real shame is in
> not taking practical measures to escape from it (Pericles, 431 BCE
> (Thucydides)).

Pericles spoke the above words during the Peloponnesian War as a reminder to grieving Athenian parents of the differences between their city-state and totalitarian Sparta. They symbolize an ethos characteristic of Athens: economic freedom. The Greek word, *Oikonomia*, originally meaning "household management," is the root word for economics. While it is erroneous to stereotype Athens and other Greek city-states and Imperial Rome (and ancient China for that matter) as having free enterprise economies as conventionally understood today, these societies were affluent because both by design and accident, powerful economic ideas were institutionalized. Lack of fertile agricultural land and growing populations forced Greeks to become what Plato called frogs on a (Mediterranean) pond. They established trading colonies in places as far flung as Egypt, the Black Sea, and the site of contemporary Lyon exporting pottery, olive oil, and other goods, using silver coins for purchases of enormous amounts of grain. Early on, evidence indicates that Athens probably became wealthier than other Greek city-states in trade by making coinage more valuable by the innovation of developing large and small denominations.

Solon, who gained power over Athens in 594 BCE, established laws that made use of economic incentives. Only fathers who taught their sons a trade were legally entitled to support from the son in old age. Solon, of an aristocratic family which lost its wealth, made his fortune as a merchant. He advanced the cause of economic freedom and battled aristocratic landowners' bias against trades people, by allegedly promulgating a law forbidding reproaching someone for the trade in which he (or she) engaged (Austin and Vidal-Naquet, 1997, p. 212).

By the mid and late fifth century BCE Athens was the commercial center of the eastern Mediterranean. Before the Peloponnesian War, Athens was the largest Greek city-state with a probable population of 305,000, including citizens, 100,000 slaves, and 25,000 free-born foreigners or metics. More than half the entire population could read and write, ensuring the necessary human capital for a variety of enterprises (Grant, 1992, p. 67). The legal system generally maintained positive institutional support for economic activity. Although a wide variety of taxes were placed on goods and services, they were low and there were few property taxes. Maritime loans enforced by written contract provided an incentive for foreign trade. Although metics and slaves couldn't own agricultural land, virtually all of the former and many of the latter engaged in commercial enterprises with metics as owners and slaves as employees at different levels.

By the fourth century BCE both metics and slaves could enter into written contracts. Also, unlike the case in some other Greek city-states, most notably Sparta, opportunities were present for economic and social mobility. Slaves, most of whom were not Athenian, could be freed and become metics and, more rarely, even citizens. Metics, who were dominant in commerce, could occasionally become citizens. One famous entrepreneur, Pasion, began his career as a slave in a bank, was freed and elevated to metic and then to citizen status. When he died, he owned a bank, a shield workshop, and extensive real estate and assets (Grant, 1992, p. 113). The economic incentives and economic freedom of Athens, in sharp contrast with Sparta, helped to make it affluent and socially stable. While metics *chose* to come to Athens and the city had virtually no slave revolts, slave revolts were frequent enough to always be a security concern in Sparta's garrison state. Athens would be absorbed by Macedonia and then later by the Roman Empire, but its golden age cannot be fully explained unless its successful economy is understood.

The Roman Empire

> Extremely low taxes encourage investment. The ordinary Roman works two days a year to pay his taxes (Fears, 2001).

Athens prospered for a little over a century with economic freedom but its widespread institutionalization in Rome's massive empire, stretching from Britain to what is now Iraq, fostered a general prosperity lasting roughly three centuries. The famous historian of freedom, Lord Acton, provoked his contemporaries when he asserted the Roman Empire did more for liberty than the earlier republic, but if economic liberty is considered as valuable as political liberty, he was correct (Fears, 2001, p. 34). In the early imperial period, although republican political liberties vanished, taxes were low, social mobility was generally prevalent, the majority of people in a multicultural polity could live the lives they choose, and a free market economy brought goods and services from the known world to Roman cities.

The Roman Empire was not a modern economy; aristocrats enjoyed legal privileges, slavery existed, technology was uneven—excellent infrastructure such as roads but below average scientific advancement compared to other civilizations such as China—and there was popular prejudice against merchants. Still, Rome, with somewhere near one million people, and numerous other cities in an empire ranging between 50 and 65 million people, maintained a legal system that was not discriminatory toward commerce, used one basic currency, and had a critical mass of literate people. Women could even own (but not sell) property, a condition unthinkable in Ancient Greece (Fears, 2001, p. 35). A large middle class lived in the cities (Grant, 1992, p. 116).

Although freeing of slaves (manumission) occurred in Athens and other Greek cities, it was much more widespread in the Roman Empire. Unlike Greece, Roman slaves could own property. They were shopkeepers, merchants, and providers of an array of services in Roman cities. Slaves could even save money and purchase their own freedom. Although people died earlier in antiquity, many slaves, and virtually all domestic slaves, could expect manumission by age 30 (Grant, 1992, p. 115).

Imperial Rome's government tread lightly on interfering with local politics and concentrated upon providing national and domestic security and maintaining a road system. The early Roman Empire had an efficient and relatively small bureaucracy. Significant numbers of prosperous citizens in Rome and other imperial cities enjoyed tourism and hotels, bookshops, and good food provided by the private sector. They also enjoyed products from China and India. Trade was particularly brisk with coastal India. Roman imports included cotton cloth, exotic animals, and spices, particularly pepper. The Romans exported glass, cosmetics, and silverware to India, but by far the biggest export was Roman gold coinage. The latter led to a cash-flow problem in the Roman Empire which the famous essayist and imperial official, Pliny the Elder, lamented in the mid-first century (Davis, 2009, pp. 9–12).

For a variety of factors including the lingering prejudice of elite Romans against merchants, the Western Roman Empire's economic fortunes waned from the fourth century CE until the fall. As the economy worsened, the once modest bureaucracy expanded and taxes rose. Various emperors attempted policies such as currency devaluation, including issuing tin-plated copper coins instead of the normal issue silver, with predictable results: rampant inflation and hoarding of silver coins.

As procuring steady supplies of food became a problem in the latter empire, wage and price controls were also attempted with Emperor Diocletian's attempt being the most far reaching. Faced with inflation that made money so worthless that barter was making a major comeback, Diocletian issued an edict in 301 CE covering well over 1,000 wages and prices (Schuettinger and Butler, 1978, pp. 19–26). The preamble to Diocletian's edict has a contemporary ring as he blamed merchants who he labeled "uncontrollable madmen" for Rome's problems (Hooper, 1979, p. 492). Diocletian's results were predictable. Temporary price stability came at the costs of hoarding, shortages, a black market, and some mob violence against merchants who exceeded set price levels. Emperor Diocletian abdicated four years after issuing the edicts, complaining of the stress of governing.

As the Western Empire neared its end, emperors frantically tried to micromanage the economy with more price controls as well as wage controls on certain occupations, which led to the army being responsible for forcing people to remain in jobs with regulated wages when they tried to find better compensation. Not only did the economic distortions grow much worse but invading Germanic tribes gained large numbers of Roman citizen sympathizers from bad policies. Rome's economic history, like that of any society, has positive and negative lessons.

Imperial China and Economic Freedom

The more prohibitions there are, the poorer the people will be (Lao Tzu, sixth century BCE).

In 1500 at the dawn of Europe's age of exploration, China had absolutely no incentive to "discover" new trade routes to Europe. Despite periods of disunification, Chinese enjoyed what was probably the world's richest economy for many years ranging from the Han Dynasty (202 BCE–220 CE) until approximately the mid eighteenth century. Although China, like Greece and Rome, was primarily an agricultural society, the empire was a world leader in technology, and enjoyed a vibrant commercial sector, some manufacturing, and domestic and international trade. China's trade surplus with Europe lasted well into the nineteenth century. The primary reasons behind China's wealth were political and legal systems that generally supported, although sometimes unintentionally, economic freedom and a culture of entrepreneurship and innovation.

Imperial Chinese institutions, beginning with the Han Dynasty, were undergirded by a combination of three belief systems: Legalism, Daoism, and Confucianism. Each had substantial components that helped to facilitate economic growth. Legalists believed that people acted from self-interest so rulers should systematically promulgate laws that tie individual self-interest to societal progress. This meant the creation of a legal framework that rewarded wealth acquisition and curtailed overly ambitious government bureaucrats from exceeding their authority regarding tax collection and private sector regulation.

Beginning with the Han dynasty, Confucianism gained favor among political elites. By the Song Dynasties (960–1279), it formed the basis of China's education system. Mastery of rigorous Confucian-based examinations, rather than birth, was the key to top positions in the Chinese bureaucracy by the millennium, ridding the empire from feudalism 400–500 years earlier than Europe and thus expanding labor market freedom. Confucianists advocated individual ethics, self-responsibility, self-cultivation, and small but effective government bureaucracy. Although Confucian scholar-bureaucrats disdained merchants as parasites, they also recognized their social usefulness and usually left them alone, while competently administering a state that generally kept taxes low, maintained a grand canal linking China's two great maritime commercial arteries, the Yellow and Yang Tse Rivers, and for much of China's history secured the famous Silk Roads linking Chinese traders with Central Asia, India, and the Mediterranean.

Libertarian ideas are evident in Daoism, the third great Chinese belief system, as David Boaz (1997) noted in his introduction to the *Libertarian Reader*. The central Daoist idea that is basic to economic freedom is that it is usually better for society if rulers stand aside and let humans get on with the daily business of living.

The institutional-legal structure described above was fully in place by the middle of the Song dynasty and, for the next several hundred years, despite dislocations and even foreign conquest, the economy prospered. Large agricultural surpluses were generated through technology and genetically resistant seeds, which in turn created rapidly expanding food supplies and markets. With the discovery of Mexico and Peru's silver mines, China became the world's largest sixteenth-century importer of the precious metal. The silver imports fueled even more economic expansion (Rawski, 2008). The Chinese exported vast quantities of tea, porcelain, and silk to Europeans.

Domestically, through local markets or major distributors who used the Grand Canal to transport food nationally, agricultural productivity advances meant that small farmers in the south's "rice bowl" were able to feed their families, pay taxes, and still market an average of 40 percent of annual yields (2004, *Asia for Educators*).

In addition to the absence of a feudal system, long-term de facto property rights also enabled Chinese farmers to prosper. Although theoretically the emperor owned all land, the institutional structures described earlier acted as a powerful check on arbitrary imperial power and farmers were left alone so they could ensure that the nation had enough to eat. Even though China's economy was agrarian-based with products like tea and silk, industries such as iron, ship-building, salt, and porcelain flourished. The government controlled sales of a few industries such as salt, but most manufacturing was less regulated. Imperial Chinese cities featured vibrant commercial activity. By 1700 an elaborate system of remittance banks existed and provided capital for merchants. Merchants deposited cash in one locale, received a remittance certificate, and used it in another part of the empire as payment for transactions (2006, *Asia for Educators*).

In the nineteenth century an elite prejudice against science and technology, a growing population problem, the Taiping rebellion, which dwarfed the American Civil War, and European encroachment weakened China's economy and in 1911 the imperial era ended. While imperial China is included in every world history textbook, explanations of the economics behind the wealth are largely non-existent.

British Colonial America

The material standard of living enjoyed by the typical white family unit in the thirteen mainland English colonies was almost certainly the highest in the world by the 1770s (Perkins, 1980, p. 145).

The approximately two-and-a-half million people who lived in Britain's American colonies created, by the standards of the day, an economic powerhouse decades before the war for independence. On that war's eve, the median annual per capita income of the free colonial population, converted into dollars, was somewhere between $65 and $165 higher than in Britain. Since the colonists were subject to lower tax rates than the British, the typical American family enjoyed a standard of living 20 percent higher than their British counterparts. In 1700, colonial gross domestic product had been 4 percent of England's; by 1770 it was 40 percent (Perkins, 1980, pp. 145, 164). The average British soldier in the French and Indian War was two inches shorter than his colonial counterpart because of differing affluence levels (McDougall, 2004, p. 123). Although slavery is a pernicious institution, even black slaves, who constituted about 20 percent of the colonial population, had a better standard of living when compared to agricultural workers in Africa and South America and on average enjoyed steady increases during the eighteenth century (Perkins, 1980, p. 78). The *vital* question in understanding both the colonial period and the roots of American affluence is how did all this happen?

The lower labor costs on the southern plantations and the British provision of virtually no-cost military protection until the last decade of the period are part of the reasons for colonial prosperity but far from the only ones. A few of the many factors responsible for most of this amazing success story include the impact of political and legal institutions upon economic activity, competitive labor markets, low taxes, and the fostering of a culture friendly to entrepreneurship and merchants.

Unlike the Conquistadores who epitomized Imperial Spain's strategy in the New World—find, extract, and transport precious metals back to the mother country—the first English settlers were subject to English legal and political traditions and different incentive structures. The sanctity of private property rights was becoming institutionalized in English political culture. Also, the almost total absence of gold and silver in English America meant that colonists did not have the precious metals extraction option. After a brief, failed experiment with common ownership of land in the Massachusetts Bay Colony in the early 1620s, founder William Bradford quickly initiated the shift from public to private ownership that made, in his 1623 words, "all hands very industrious" (Schug et al., 2006, p. 39). Cheap land made private property ownership and its accrued benefits even more important in the American colonies than in England. By the latter colonial period a majority of American farmers outright owned and worked their land and tenancy rates were low by European standards. In England, absentee landed gentry owned most land, which was worked by tenants with few economic incentives for productivity. Farm owner operators of 40 acres or more of farms only held about one-quarter of English farm land (Perkins, 1980, pp. 41–42).

Labor was a scarce commodity in most of the 13 colonies and the colonial population expanded as Europeans left the old world for economic opportunities. Although large-scale manufacturing, with the major exceptions of shipbuilding and iron, was never a major part of the colonial economy, artisans and merchants found the colonies, and particularly the growing urban centers, attractive. For silver-smiths, candle-makers, and blacksmiths not only were fees and wages on average 30 to 100 percent higher than for identical work in Britain, but the absence of an institutionalized guild system meant that unlike in Britain, an aspiring artisan had more freedom to produce goods or services (Perkins, 1980, p. 82).

Farmers, artisans, and merchants were also richer than their counterparts in Britain for yet another reason; Americans had more disposable income because of tax rates that were among the lowest of all organized governments. Until the now infamous tax increases of the 1760s, British colonists paid a little under 20 percent on average of the rates of the mother country. Port cities such as Boston and Philadelphia tended to have the highest colonial tax rates, but residents in those cities only paid a total of 4–5 percent of annual incomes in taxes (Perkins, 1980, pp. 123–125).

Colonial economic success stories are impressive. New Englanders were adroit at both building ships and transporting goods throughout the British Empire as well as to other countries. The New England colonies literally became a world shipping power (North, 1966, p. 40). Foreign trade accounted for 10–12 percent of colonial economic output with New England business concerns selling dried fish to southern Europe and a variety of goods including horses, pine boards, cattle, and candles to the Caribbean. The middle colonies also exported products to southern Europe and the West Indies including bread, flour, wheat, and salted pork. A variety of merchants operated in American cities selling imports from Britain and other European countries as well as domestically produced merchandise (Perkins, 1980, pp. 17–36). Southern colonists exported tobacco and indigo as well. Although with the exception of iron, large-scale manufacturing was rare in America, more and more merchants, planters, and professionals were experimenting with manufacturing as side lights by the end of the period and investments ranged from hat to candle factories.

In part, impressive levels of colonial growth and affluence were generated because from the start, there was no entrenched aristocracy who looked down upon business. The culture of entrepreneurship flourished in the colonies. Even southern planters might engage in commercial farming, also practice law, and dabble in investing in export ventures. Merchants enjoyed high status and unlike in Europe, had a much easier time becoming involved in government. The U.S. tradition of respect for merchants and business leadership in politics pre-dates the founding of the nation as does the American tradition of achieving affluence and being proud of it.

The British Industrial Revolution: A Dark Time?

> There is however, one supreme myth which more than any other has served to discredit the economic system to which we owe our present-day civilization.... It is the legend of the deterioration of the position of the working classes in consequence of the rise of capitalism (Hayek, 1963, p. 10).

Nowhere is Hayek's above assertion more valid than with the case of the British Industrial Revolution. In 2004 research for a Fordham Foundation project focusing upon world history texts, the author examined the treatment of this seminal event in five leading high school world history texts (Ravitch, 2004). Typically, coverage is a combination of a few pages on impressive advances in technology and a greater number of pages on the horrid conditions of the British working class in general and children in particular. Consider a "student interactive" page from a leading text telling the story of a small boy who left his rural family to join an uncle in a textile factory.

Once students have read the account and seen a graphic portrait of a boy frantically working with a menacing looking adult watching, they are given this "portfolio" assignment.

> After a 12 hour day at the mill, you decided to write a letter to your family. In your letter, describe your new job and say whether you want to keep working here in Manchester or go back home to the farm (Ellis and Esler, 2003, p. 507).

This typical, probably unintentional, distortion of the Industrial Revolution is an educational one, but misleading examples about the event abound in literature and cinema. Perhaps no topic in economic history has been so misrepresented. What were the Industrial Revolution's economic effects in Britain when it was occurring? What was the range of opinions about industrialization at the time? How does an economic analysis of housing for the poor and child factory labor influence one's understanding of the Industrial Revolution?

The general short-term effect of the Industrial Revolution is that it improved the standard of living of most British people, including the working urban poor. In the early part of the nineteenth century and for decades afterward, new technology and organization resulted in greatly expanded production of an array of goods, beginning with cotton textiles. International trade increased, British population grew but wages did not drop and in many industries they increased. Price levels declined because of better productivity and increased trade. Ordinary British citizens, including all but the poorest of the poor, could attain a vast amount of new products for the first time including comfortable clothing, tea, coffee, sugar, clocks, handkerchiefs, boots, and wheat bread. They could eat meat, fish, and poultry regularly and not just for special occasions. Even among the urban lower middle and working classes, savings banks, popular newspapers, pamphlets, and the construction of new Protestant churches attested to rising standards of living (Ashton, cited in Hayek, 1963, pp. 137–155). Factory growth also provided employment stability at higher wages than poor people could find in rural areas and they flocked to the growing cities.

Certainly dangerous and unsanitary conditions existed in many smaller factories and certain factory operatives, particularly hand-loom workers, were at risk. But even while events were unfolding, politics, naivety, and widespread ignorance of the actual lives of the working poor as well as of economics, caused profound misimpressions of what was actually occurring to become conventional wisdom. Opponents of industrialization included Tory landowners, with their deep prejudices against tradesmen and factory owners, and Victorian social reformers.

There were exceptions, particularly among Victorian reformers, but majorities of both groups and their supportive upper-middle- and upper-class publics usually had never set foot in a factory. Tories were ready to believe, quite possibly because of legitimate fears of a depleted low-cost agricultural work force, stories about horrible conditions in factories. One result was acceptance of a sensational 1831–1832 report to Parliament that overexaggerated adverse conditions for children even though subsequent reports in 1833 and 1834 evidentially refuted it (Hutt, cited in Hayek, 1963, pp. 159–160). Content based upon the first "Sadler" Committee report still remain conventional history text wisdom. Although Victorian reformers, especially those who visited factories, pointed out legitimate problems, many also thought the factories were bad for workers, including children, because they gave employees enough income to consume too much tea and sweets and encouraged young girls to buy dresses from shops instead of virtuously making their own clothes! Also, opposition to a changing economy coincidentally occurred during the revival of British literary romanticism. This meant novelists, most prominently Charles Dickens, were able to add fuel to the rhetorical fires through poignant narratives.

In contemporary texts and popular culture, the Industrial Revolution and greedy landlords receive exclusive blame for cities characterized by terrible housing for the working poor. These allegations ignore important developments shortly before and during the early years of industrialization that affected the supply and quality of housing for the poor. In the latter decade of the eighteenth century and the first decade and a half of the nineteenth, imperial Britain engaged in a long and costly war with Napoleon. The British government

commandeered or paid attractive prices for many of the raw materials, bricks and timber for example, used in home construction. The
result was a housing shortage in Britain's cities that most adversely
impacted the range of choices for poor immigrants from the rural
areas. As small builders struggled to meet pent up and increasing
demand for houses, government placed a wide range of taxes on
numerous products to raise much-needed war funds and, later, to pay
off the national debt. For example, homebuilders and landlords,
often the same people, were responsible for paying a tax for each
window in a house. Home construction entrepreneurs who built
inexpensive homes, many of whom had businesses with only two to
five employees, were often capital starved, suffered high bankruptcy
rates, and thus had every possible incentive to cut costs. Hence the
government, not builders, was at least partially responsible for what
one historian has described as "a price on light and air" (Ashton,
cited in Hayek, 1963, p. 50).

When the question of child labor is analyzed from an economic
perspective a different perspective emerges than one of simple degra-
dation and misery. Contrary to the perceptions of many romantics,
working in a factory was a better alternative for poor children and
their parents than others that existed at the time. Educational opportunities were extremely scarce and even Peter Gaskell, a prominent
Victorian reformer and no friend of factories, argued that factories
were a better choice for poor children than the streets or remaining at
home unattended during the day. An examination of the charge that
poor children that worked in factories were puny and deformed compared to poor children who didn't was empirically refuted in the
Parliament-commissioned 1833 and 134 reports (Hutt, cited in
Hayek, 1963, pp. 168, 174). Rural work, which children regularly did,
was for the most part much more physically taxing than the relatively
light work to which they were assigned in factories. Although the
long-term consequences because of a growth in educational opportunities were beneficial for many poor children, the unintended short-
term consequences of the first child labor laws meant less money for
poor families and an abrupt interruption of behaviors and skills that
children were learning in the workplace that would help them keep
employment as adults (Hutt, in Hayek, 1963, pp. 180–183).

Perceptions of the costs and benefits of the British Industrial Revolution may very well be the single topic most characterized by economic illiteracy. Perhaps the situation may one day change.

The U.S. and the World Depression

We will not have any more crashes in our time (Keynes, 1927).

The U.S. Depression dramatically affected a generation and created public "memories" about the role of government that often resulted in bad economic policies in ensuing decades. The events of the 1930s left an indelible impact on most Americans alive at the time. In 1933, at its depths, 25 percent of all workers were unemployed. After a moderate 1935–1937 recovery, by 1938, unemployment soared to over 19 percent and was still at almost 15 percent in 1940. Full employment would only come after the beginning of World War II (Smiley, 2008). Why did the depression occur? What were the effects of government policies intended to fight it? How did impressions of the event influence later government economic policy?

The events leading up to the American Depression had both domestic and international causes. Domestically, a boom in stocks caused their overvaluation. Eventually the "bubble" burst in October 1929 with the Wall Street Crash. This event, however, only triggered the depression and was not a long-term cause of it, or probably of its exceptional U.S. longevity. Since the end of World War I, foreign investors and governments were allowed to buy gold from the United States, which remained on the gold standard and owned approximately 40 percent of the monetary version of the precious metal. In 1928, investors and governments in countries with unstable currencies bought large amounts of gold from the United States. The Federal Reserve Board, in an attempt to stem the gold outflow, raised the discount rate it charged member banks, pushing up interest rates. Although the move was intended to incentivize foreigners to buy American bonds instead of gold, the policy also raised interest rates throughout the American economy, which discouraged business spending (Schug et al., 2006, p. 352).

The Hoover administration attempted a number of policies including first reducing taxes and then, when government surpluses turned to deficits, raising them which further discouraged business growth as did the administration and private sector's notion that keeping wages high would encourage spending. Less growth meant higher unemployment and major reductions in aggregate spending (Smiley, 2008). Hoover's successor, Franklin Roosevelt, initiated a plethora of policies to combat the slump; some of which were effective and some with serious unintended negative consequences. The more successful policies included Roosevelt's 1933 bank holiday and taking America off the gold standard, which restored American confidence in a banking system that was collapsing.

Government programs such as the Works Project Administration and the Federal Emergency Relief Act created temporary government jobs that increased aggregate demand and spending (Schug et al., pp. 366–367). However, two federal programs, the Agricultural Adjustment Act and the National Recovery Act, made the economy worse. Policy-makers based both programs on the assumption that overproduction was the cause of low prices and if production was curtailed prices would rise and producers would earn more. The AAA slaughtered six million pigs, when many Americans were hungry, and paid cotton farmers to destroy a quarter of planted crops, which gave landowners but not tenants economic relief. The National Recovery Act employed the same policy with major industries as the government coordinated production. The effect of both programs was to make some agricultural products and industrial products too expensive for many Americans to buy and to increase unemployment on farms and in factories (Smiley, 2008).

Even though full employment did not occur until World War II, because of Roosevelt's charisma and numerous high-profile government initiatives most ordinary Americans believed his policies were responsible for ending the depression. These policies were partly based on the ideas of economist John Maynard Keynes who perpetuated the notion that policy-makers could manipulate the economy like a machine. The basic Keynesian notion was that government should spend less in good times, building a surplus, and increase spending in bad times to prime the economic pump. For decades after the 1930s, Keynesian economics, which ignored perpetual incentives for governments to always spend, was conventional wisdom. Eventually, the economic doldrums of the 1970s and early 1980s ended, for at least a large segment of the general public and policy-makers, a faith in the efficacy of significant widespread government management of the economy.

The United States and the Great Recession

Certainly, the question of government's role in the economy, always an ongoing source of debate, is still relevant today. What lessons, for example, might be drawn from a comparison of government policies before and during the Great Depression of the 1930s and government policies preceding and after the Great Recession of 2007–2010?

The probable causes of the Great Recession were quite different from the causes of the Great Depression. The seeds for the contemporary collapse of the housing market were planted in the early 1990s. The passage of the 1992 Federal Housing Enterprises Financial Safety and Soundness Act, for example, intended to make homes affordable to moderate and low-income populations had the unintended economic consequence of increasing the number of borrowers with poor credit and assets who could obtain home loans. Mortgage bankers were under pressure from the Community Reinvestment Act to provide mortgages to individuals who did not meet traditional lending standards but also had an incentive because of the law to avoid risk through selling these questionable loans to government-sponsored enterprises such as Fannie Mae (Federal National Mortgage Association) and Freddie Mac (Federal Home Mortgage Corporation). Fannie Mae and Freddie Mac took on more than $6 trillion of single family loans from 1992 to 2008. Efforts in 2005 to rein in high-risk, government-sanctioned lending were brushed aside by Congressional leaders.

The changes in lending standards and the expansion of Fannie and Freddie coincided with the Federal Reserve keeping its key interest rate—the federal funds rate—too low for too long. Low interest rates encouraged households to take on large amounts of debt. All of this—high-risk lending and low interest rates—was just fine as long as housing prices increased. Housing prices were relatively stable during the 1990s. They began to rise toward the end of the 1990s and between January 2002 and mid-2006, they skyrocketed. But beginning in 2006, the boom turned into a bust and the housing prices declined throughout 2007 and 2008.

There are three lessons that we can learn from the Great Depression. The first is to avoid poor monetary policy. Earlier in this chapter, it was pointed out that the Federal Reserve, in an effort to shore up confidence in the U.S. dollar, raised interest rates in the middle of a recession. In addition, the Federal Reserve failed to act as the lender of last resort to banks. It allowed thousands of banks to fail thus shrinking the money supply and causing credit to dry up. Clearly, the Federal Reserve today has learned this Depression-era lesson very well. So far it has kept interest rates low and rescued troubled banks and other financial institutions. The Federal Reserve acted swiftly in 2008 and 2009 and poured billions of dollars into the financial system. The financial system did not collapse.

The second lesson from the Great Depression is to avoid poor fiscal policy. The Hoover administration increased income taxes in an effort to balance the budget. The policy resulted in further reduced consumer spending. Here, contemporary government policy appears to be ignoring lessons from the past. Several taxes will be increased under the health care legislation signed into law in early 2010. Add to that the new income tax increases. The tax-rate reductions passed during the administration of President Bush expire at the end of 2010. Presuming no new federal legislation, the top personal income tax rate will increase from 35 to 39 percent and the dividend and capital gains tax rates will rise from 15 to 20 percent. Moreover, the estate tax is set to end in 2010 but to reappear in 2011 as a 55 percent tax on inherited wealth exceeding $1 million.

Increased spending after passage of numerous new government programs under the New Deal created uncertainty and most likely delayed the economic recovery. Business leaders were reluctant to invest in new equipment and hire new employees in the face of widespread and unknown changes in the regulatory environment. Once again, today's government policy seems to be ignoring lessons from the past. The year-long debate regarding changes in health care insurance, prolonged debates regarding tax increases and major overhauls in the regulation of financial institutions almost certainly creates uncertainty and delays a full recovery.

The third lesson is for government to avoid protectionist trade policies. The Smoot-Hawley Tariff Act of 1930 (discussed in Chapter 3) hurt exporting domestic businesses and consumers of imports thus reducing the standards of living among the United States and its trade partners. Here, Washington leaders once again appear willing to learn from the events of the Great Depression. Thus far, the United States has resisted large-scale efforts to undermine international trade. However, the United States has negotiated trade agreements with Colombia, Panama, and South Korea but has so far failed to act on them.

Conclusion: Teaching Resources

Numerous resources are available to assist teachers in integrating economics into world and U.S. history courses. Table 10.1 offers several websites, curriculum guides, books, and audio courses developed by excellent scholars and teachers. These resources contain content and classroom activities that are particularly applicable for high school and university survey level history instructors.

Educators should think "outside the box" when considering entries included in the table. For example, teachers typically don't think of audio resources as good pedagogical tools for adolescents. However, Professor Rufus Fears, the single-most popular lecturer who works with the *Teaching Company*, clearly understands the importance of economic freedom and dynamically conveys that importance in ways that will most assuredly appeal to many young people. This is true not just in the case of the entry in Table 10.1, but applies to other series Fears has developed for the *Teaching Company*.

Chapter 1 of Gwartney, Stroup, and Lee's *Common Sense Economics* should perhaps be required reading in history as well as economics classes because it may very well be the best-written explanation of

Table 10.1 Pedagogical Resources

Education About Asia website. Ann Arbor MI: Association for Asian Studies. Retrieved on November 18, 2009, from: www.asian-studies.org/EAA.

Several economic history articles are available on the website of this journal for teachers.

Columbia University. *Asia for Educators* website. Retrieved on November 18, 2009, from: http://afe.easia.columbia.edu.

Components on China and Europe, the Silk Roads, and the Song dynasty graphically demonstrate imperial China's economic freedom.

Davis, R. (2010). *Global India Circa 100 CE: South Asia in Early World History.*
The chapter on merchants and trade illustrates the long-term power of Indian commerce.

Fears, J.R. (2001). "Freedom in the Roman Empire." *Philosophy & Intellectual History: A History of Freedom Part 1* (audio series with study guide). Chantilly, VA: The Teaching Company.

This series, and several others by a master teaching professor, are highly recommended for students of economic freedom.

Gordon, S. (2008). *When Asia Was the World.* Philadelphia, PA: Da Capo Press.

The author of this featured History Book Club work includes several chapters that are illustrative of Asia's economic dynamism from 500 to 1500 CE.

Gwartney, J., Stroup, R.L., and Lee, D.R. (2005). *Common Sense Economics.* New York: St. Martin's Press.

The best introduction to basic economics available in print.

McCorkle, S., Meszaros, B.T., Odorzynski, S.J., Schug, M.C., Watts, M., and Horwich, G. (2002). "Lesson Four: Sparta, Athens, Cuba, and the United States: Ancient and Modern Examples of Command and Market Economies." *Focus: Economic Systems.* New York: National Council on Economic Education.

This is an excellent lesson that illustrates economic incentives don't change over time.

Public Broadcasting Company. *The Roman Empire in the 1st Century*. Retrieved on November 18, 2009, from: www.pbs.org/empires/romans/educators/index.html.

Several video segments illustrating Rome's wealth and social system are available online.

Reed, L. "Child Labor and the Industrial Revolution." Midland, MI: Mackinac Center for Public Policy. Retrieved on December 3, 2009, from: http://www.mackinac.org/3879.

Economic analyses of the Industrial Revolution suitable for classroom use appear virtually non-existent. This Lawrence Reed essay that originally appeared in *The Freeman* is an exception.

Roberts, J.T. and Barrett, T. (2004). *The Ancient Greek World*. New York: Oxford University Press.

This publication, written for ninth-graders, is a good general text and resource. There are also volumes in the same series on Rome and imperial China.

Schug, M.C., Caldwell, J., and Ferrarini, T.H. (2006). *Focus: Understanding Economics in United States History*. New York: National Council on Economic Education.

This comprehensive guide is an essential pedagogical tool for any U.S. History instructor.

economics generalizations currently in print. It contains *no* supply or demand curves, mathematical formulae, or tables laden with statistics, yet is a quintessential primer in basic economics.

Finally, apparently given the almost total absence of teaching materials on the British Industrial Revolution that employ economic analysis, anyone who teaches world history should read Lawrence Read's essay on child labor (publication details also included in Table 10.1).

References

Austin, M.M. and Vidal-Naquet, P. (1997). *Economic and Social History of Ancient Greece: An Introduction.* Berkeley, CA: University of California Press.

Boaz, D. (1997). *The Libertarian Reader: Classic and Contemporary Writings from Lao Tzu to Milton Friedman.* New York: Free Press.

Davis, R. (2010). *Global India Circa 100 CE: South Asia in Early World History.* Ann Arbor, MI: Association for Asian Studies.

Ellis, E. and Esler, E. (2003). *World History: Connections to Today.* Upper Saddle River, NJ: Pearson/Prentice Hall.

Engen, D.T. (2004). "The Economy of Ancient Greece." *EH.Net Encyclopedia*, edited by Robert Whaples. Retrieved on November 18, 2009, from: http://eh.net/encyclopedia/article/engen.greece.

Fears, J.R. (2001). "Freedom in the Roman Empire." *Philosophy & Intellectual History: A History of Freedom Part 1* [audio series with study guide]. Chantilly, VA: The Teaching Company.

Garnsey, P. and Saller, R. (1987). *The Roman Empire: Economy, Society and Culture.* Berkeley, CA: University of California Press.

Grant, M. (1992). *A Social History of Greece and Rome.* New York: Charles Scriber's Sons.

Gwartney, J., Stroup, R., and Lee, D. (2005). *Common Sense Economics: What Everyone Should Know about Wealth and Prosperity.* New York: St. Martin's Press.

Hayek, F.A. (Ed.) (1963). *Capitalism and the Historians.* Chicago, IL: University of Chicago Press.

Hooper, F. (1979). *Roman Realities.* Detroit, MI: Wayne State University Press.

McDougall, W. (2004). *Freedom Just Around the Corner: A New American History 1585–1828.* New York: HarperCollins.

North, D.C. (1966). *Growth and Welfare in the American Past: A New Economic History.* Englewood Cliffs, NJ: Prentice-Hall, Inc.

Perkins, E.J. (1980). *The Economy of Colonial America.* New York: Columbia University Press.

Ravitch, D. (Ed.) (2004). *A Consumer's Guide to High School History Textbooks.* Washington, DC: The Thomas B. Fordham Foundation.

Rawski, T. (2008). "Economic Influence in China's Relations with the West." Foreign Policy Research Institute. Retrieved on November 18, 2009, from: www.fpri.org/footnotes/1309.200808.rawski.economicinfluencechinawest. html.

Schuettinger, R.L. and Butler, E.F. (1978). *Forty Centuries of Wage and Price Controls: How Not To Fight Inflation.* Washington, DC: The Heritage Foundation.

Schug, M.C., Caldwell, J., and Ferrarini, T.H. (2006). *Focus: Understanding Economics in United States History.* New York: National Council on Economic Education.

Smiley, G. (2008). "Great Depression." Library of Economics and Liberty. Retrieved on November 18, 2009, from: www.econlib.org/library/Enc/ GreatDepression.html.

PART III

RESEARCH FINDINGS IN ECONOMIC EDUCATION

11

Best Economic Education Practices for Children

Phillip J. VanFossen

The chapters in this volume are mainly focused on economic education at the secondary level—but how much economics do students know as they walk in the door to those classes? How much should they know from economic education at the primary (K–3) and intermediate (4–6) grade levels? This chapter will spend a good deal of time examining the relevant literature on K–6 economic education in order to build a case for it. Specifically, this examination will pose and answer three questions:

- Can young children learn and apply economic concepts?
- If they can learn such concepts, should these be taught in the elementary school curriculum?
- If they can learn such concepts and we deem these concepts worth including in the K–6 curriculum, how should we teach for economic understanding among young children?

The sections that follow will provide a synopsis of the relevant literature designed to answer each of these questions. The section devoted to the third question will also include some detailed examples of teaching practices and materials that have proved to be promising for teaching economic concepts to young learners. Finally, the chapter will conclude with a call to reexamine priorities in K–6 social studies education and to focus more explicitly on teaching for economic literacy at these grade levels.

Can Young Children Learn and Apply Economic Concepts?

Do young children have an understanding of the economic world around them and their role in that world? If so, is it possible to expand this understanding through developmentally appropriate economic education? Based on a reading of the relevant literature, the clear answer to both these questions is yes. Indeed, research has confirmed that children as young as five can—and do—learn basic economic concepts such as scarcity and opportunity cost (Schug and Birkey, 1985; Kourilsky, 1977; Robinson, 1963).

One early study of young children's economic learning was conducted by Larkins and Shaver (1969) on students who had completed the *Families at Work* curriculum of economic education pioneer Lawrence Senesh (1964). Following instruction that used Senesh's elementary-grade textbook *Families at Work*, Larkins and Shaver tested over 650 first-grade students in four different studies and concluded that because "the results were consistent in all studies, the evidence indicated that first-grade children can learn at least some of the content" in an elementary economics curriculum (p. 961).

Sosin et al. (1997) used a quasi-experimental design to examine students' economic learning in seven elementary classes between grades 3 and 6. Experimental group teachers in the study had special training in economic education; the teachers in the 11 control groups did not. The authors determined that the elementary-age students in the experimental groups learned significantly more economics than students in the control groups and that "not only can all [economic] concept groups be taught in elementary grades, but third and fourth grade students can apparently achieve posttest scores comparable to sixth grade students in one year of instruction" (1997, p. 119). In describing the results of the Sosin et al. study, Laney and Schug (1998, p. 14) stated: "the evidence seems clear: teach them [i.e., elementary-age students] economics, and they will learn."

Over the last five decades, a body of research has attempted to describe the process by which children develop this understanding of their economic world and how they learn economic content (Miller and VanFossen, 2008). In many of these studies (e.g., Berti, 1988; Schug and Birkey, 1985; Berti and Bombi, 1981) children were interviewed in order to collect data about their understanding of a particular economic concept and to attempt to describe the kind of "spontaneous concept development" that happens as children experience the economic world around them (Laney, 1993, p. 228). Schug and Walstad (1991) suggested that results from these studies indicated that children's economic thinking moved through "a series of levels or stages similar to those described by Jean Piaget" (p. 414). More recent research (e.g., Diez-Martinez and Ochoa, 2003; Webley and Plaisier, 1998; Laney et al., 1996) has confirmed the presence of this stage development.

A study by Schug and Lephardt (1992) illustrated the stage development of children's economic knowledge. The authors randomly selected 67 children in grades one, six, and 11. These children were asked questions about international trade and their responses were transcribed, and the researchers then classified the student responses. The results suggested that children's reasoning about international trade was characterized by increasingly sophisticated responses. The stages of development identified were: (1) nations trade because "people want to have things from other countries"; (2) nations trade because each nation benefits from the trade; or (3) nations "buy goods and services from other nations because the cost is less" (Schug, 1994, pp. 27–28).

Another theme that has been explored in this literature is that young children often have misconceptions about their economic world, misconceptions that can—and should—be addressed by economic education. Miller and VanFossen (2008), in their comprehensive review of research on economic education generally, concluded that "a number of studies have found that children often have significant misconceptions about basic economic concepts that remain if uncorrected" (p. 292). Laney and Schug (1998) stated that "it comes as no surprise that a child's thinking about the economic world differs from that of the economist" and went on to conclude that this does not "stop children from explaining their often ill-conceived economic theories to the classroom teacher" (p. 14). These misconceptions included children's belief that (1) work and income are not connected; (2) the price tag size determines a good's price; (3) the value of money comes from its size; and (4) property is owned by those who are near it (Schug and Birkey, 1985; Kourilsky, 1993; Laney and Schug, 1998).

Why Should Young Children Learn Economics?

Elementary-age students engage in decision-making on a daily, if not hourly, basis. Such decisions commonly include whether to pack their lunch or buy it, whether to play kickball or soccer at recess, whether to do homework or play outside, whether to "friend" someone on Facebook, and so on. While—on their face—these decisions might not seem "economic" in nature, they are. The discipline of economics is often referred to as the "science of analyzing decisions and decision-making" and so whenever children "make choices, those choices can be examined using an economic way of thinking" (VanFossen, 2003, p. 90). Meszaros (2010, p. 4) summarizes the case for early economic education this way:

> Economics is the study of making decisions given limited resources. Young children live in an economic world and bring economic knowledge into the classroom. They learn early they can't have everything they want. They are very aware that choices must be made. What to wear, what electronic game to play, what to eat, what television show to watch, how to spend their money and what to do with their time are but a few of the decisions they face on a daily basis. Too often students don't understand why it is necessary for them to make choices. Nor do they realize that every choice involves a cost. Some erroneously believe they will have everything they want when they are adults. Others think the only reason they face scarcity is because adults are unfair or others impose constraints upon them.

Indeed, some economic educators see the application of economic decision-making as "the most important economic concept for elementary school students to learn" because the development of "our children into adult decision-makers depends greatly on their acquisition of the concept" (Laney, 1993, p. 99). Schug (1985) made a strong case for the importance of early economic education because it "introduces young people to a highly useful way of thinking about basic issues and making personal decisions" (p. 6). Writing in a special issue of the Minneapolis Federal Reserve Bank's *The Region*, former President of the Council on Economic Education Robert Duvall concluded that economic literacy was every bit as vital as reading literacy (Stern, 1999).

As research on the stage development of children's economic knowledge suggests, older students can grasp more sophisticated economic ideas than very young children. What this research also implies, however, is that for these later stages of understanding to be reached, early concept introduction is required. One of the leading architects of early childhood economic education was Purdue University economics professor Lawrence Senesh. Senesh's *Our Working World* textbook series, first published in 1963, was among the first elementary school textbooks to have explicit lessons on economic content. In fact, economics formed the "central perspective" of Senesh's systems approach to elementary school social studies (Harrington and Rueff, 2000, p. 11). Senesh's textbooks hinged on a spiral curriculum (Taba et al., 1971) that focused on five "big ideas" in economics for which "new topics should be introduced related to the same ideas at each succeeding grade, only with increasing depth and understanding" (Harrington and Rueff, 2000, p. 13). The obvious implication of this approach to economic education is that concepts (e.g., Senesh's "big ideas") must be introduced as early in the curriculum as possible, if students are to increase their understanding at each and every grade level.

A more pragmatic rationale for early economic education may be seen in the ever-increasing role elementary-age children play in our national (and international) economy. Greenspan (2003) reported the results of a Harris Interactive/Youth Pulse poll that determined that pre-teens (ages 8 to 12) in the United States were responsible for $19.1 billion in direct spending. However, the amount of indirect economic activity that young people influence may be even greater. A decade ago, McNeal (1999) estimated that children under 12 influenced between $400 and $500 billion in annual family purchases. Evidence from a more recent Harris poll indicated that:

> 75% of online 8 to 12 year olds influence which groceries the family buys, almost half (49%) influence their parents clothing choices, and 7 in 10 said they have a major influence on where the family decides to go on vacation (Harris Interactive, 2000).

Clearly, young children have a tremendous economic impact and are already making important economic and consumption decisions—all the more reason to prepare them for a lifetime of such decision-making.

How Should We Teach for Economic Understanding among Young Children?

The research literature is clear that young children can—and should—learn the key economic concepts that will help them develop economic understanding. In order to accomplish this goal, however, it is important to consider what we know about how young children learn economics. First, it is essential that we help young students overcome the economic misunderstandings and misconceptions they bring to the classroom.

Schug (1994) highlighted the importance of addressing the "confusion many students have" about economics and the economy and the need to focus on key economic ideas (in the same vein as Senesh) and to "teach them thoroughly, drawing heavily on personal and family economic experiences of students" (p. 32). Laney and Schug (1998, pp. 15–16) stressed that the methods used by elementary teachers were crucial to overcoming the misconceptions held by students:

> Teachers can deepen their students' understanding of economics by assisting them in replacing their intuitive constructions of social knowledge with constructions based on disciplined inquiry. Failing to do so means that naive understandings simply persist and may become more difficult to dislodge later. For example, it is easy to imagine a child correctly completing a test that requires knowing the definition of opportunity cost. It may well be the case, however, that the child has no sense of how to apply the concept in the real world. When asked what is the cost of staying up late to watch television, the child might say there is no cost. Students believe that watching network television is, of course, free.

Next, it is important to recognize that elementary teachers' approach to teaching economic concepts matters. Laney and Schug (1998) were adamant that young children's economic learning must be "meaningful and memorable" and that "experience-based instructional approaches can contribute significantly" to developing students' economic understanding (p. 16). Further, these authors reminded teachers that while experiential learning such as simulations and games is often preferable, simply exposing students to a concept once is not likely to have a long-lasting cognitive impact and that teachers "may need to focus students' attention on the concept to be learned through some more direct form of instruction, such as a teacher-lead debriefing session" (p. 16).

Laney (1993) compared the economic learning of two first-grade classrooms: one taught using such an experiential approach to economic education and one a more traditional approach. Laney found that the experiential group retained more knowledge of the ten basic economics concepts taught and concluded that "economic concepts appear to be more meaningful and more memorable when real-life experiences with these concepts are provided" (p. 236). Laney and Schug (1998, p. 16) summarized guidelines for teachers (drawn from Kourilsky, 1983) who wished to provide such an experience-based economic education:

- Introduce new economic ideas through real-life rather than vicarious experiences.
- Provide students with active rather than passive economic experiences.
- Let students bear the consequences of their economic decisions.
- Use direct, teacher-led instruction to focus students' attention on the economic ideas to be gleaned from their own real-world experiences and to correct economic misconceptions.
- Reinforce experience-based economic learning with vicarious experiences, using role-play, stories, pictures, games, and various cooperative learning tasks.

Other researchers have studied the impact of particular economic education materials—specifically audio-visual materials—on elementary student economic learning. Morgan (1991), for example, examined the impact of the video series *Econ and Me* (Agency for Instructional Technology, 1989) on 300 first, second, and third graders. Using a pre- and post-test design, Morgan measured students' economic knowledge of five basic economic concepts (goods and services, producers and consumers, scarcity, opportunity cost, and productive resources) before and after direct instruction using the video series. Morgan concluded that students who had participated in lessons using the video series increased their post-test scores significantly, implying increased knowledge of these concepts.

Researchers have also studied the impact of teaching economics using art and art concepts. Laney et al. (1996) explored the relationship between fifth-graders' ideas about art and economic concepts. Laney et al. studied classes of fifth-graders before and after an integrated art–economics unit. Data analysis indicated that—on average—students increased their understanding of both art *and* economic concepts. The authors indicated that, of the two, however, the student learning of the economic concepts was actually better than for art concepts. These results seem to support the claim that integrating economic content within a study of other disciplines can help facilitate young children's deeper learning of these concepts.

Certain teacher variables can also influence young children's economic learning. Perhaps the most critical of these is teacher training and background in economics and economic education. Elementary teachers tend to have little or no formal university coursework in economics as well as little professional development training on teaching economics to young children. Yet, as Michael Watts (2005) has stressed: "At both the elementary and secondary levels, students of teachers *who know more economics*, who spend more time teaching economics, and who use good instructional materials, learn more economics" (p. 1; emphasis added). It is difficult to teach an idea without knowing it, and so elementary teachers' general lack of knowledge of economics implies they teach less of it and—if they are teaching it—the potential for inaccurate teaching increases. Perhaps nowhere can the consequences of this general lack of economic knowledge be more clearly seen than in the long-standing debate over whether the concept of "needs" exists in economics. Kindergarten teachers often implement a lesson in which students define the concept "needs," distinguish needs from "wants," and then categorize various objects as a "need" or a "want." These are often enjoyable lessons for young students. The problem here lies in the fact that economics does not have a concept called "needs." This is because it is an artificial distinction. Both filet mignon and ramen noodles are food (a "need"), but clearly one goes well beyond meeting the minimum calorie requirements to survive. Where to draw the line? Economists don't bother, as they only discuss the idea of economic "wants." As Gallagher (2010) pointed out:

> There is no mention of the term *need* in the Council for Economic Education's <u>National Voluntary Economics Standards</u>. Standard One on *scarcity* states that "Students will understand that: Productive resources are limited. Therefore, people cannot have all the goods and services they want; as a result, they must choose some things and give up others." It goes on to define *economic wants* as "desires that can be satisfied by consuming a good, service, or leisure activity." *Need* is not an economics concept. Economics is about making choices that use one's resources efficiently, effectively, and thoughtfully in order to acquire the *wants* one values most (p. 15; emphasis in original).

If elementary teachers knew more economics, would their students learn more economics? Sosin et al. (1997) examined the impact of focused teacher training and professional development on the economic learning of students. The study design collected data from nine elementary classrooms (grades three through six) and 11 control group classrooms (same grade levels). The experimental group consisted of elementary teachers in a graduate course focused on professional development designed to foster the integration of economic concepts into their classrooms. Teachers in the control group taught no economic content in their classrooms for the duration of the study. Students in experimental classrooms (where economics was explicitly taught by teachers trained to do so) scored significantly higher than students in the classrooms of control group teachers. In fact, post-test scores from students in the experimental groups were—on average—more than double those from students in the control groups. Most importantly, however, all students in the experimental groups learned economic concepts, and those students who were taught more economics, learned more economics. The implications for these findings are clear: students taught economics by teachers who know economics—and who know how to teach it—are more successful at learning economic concepts.

Promising Practices in Elementary Economic Education

The evidence seems clear: young children can learn economics content and the acquisition of that knowledge is a function of—among other things—the economic content background and experience of the teacher, how the economic content is taught, and the quality of the instructional materials used. How then to foster successful economic education in the elementary grades? The remainder of this chapter explores five promising practices in K–5 economic education: (1) using children's literature to teach economic concepts; (2) using Internet-based lessons; (2) using the *Mini-Economy* classroom simulation; (4) integrating economic concepts into other content areas (e.g., mathematics) and teaching financial literacy using materials such as the *Financial Fitness for Life* curriculum.

Using children's literature to teach economics concepts. Economic educators have long promoted the use of children's literature to teach economic concepts (Kehler, 1998) and such an approach has long been widely accepted as a promising practice in economic education. According to Rodgers et al. (2007), such an approach has been "gaining in popularity" and it is becoming more common "for teachers to integrate literature with economics content into classroom time devoted primarily to reading aloud to children or to reading instruction with a relatively short discussion of the main economic ideas" (p. 47). Rodgers et al. also argued that "primary-grade students can gain exposure to a wide range of the economic concepts contained in state standards if teachers use reading strategies that embrace children's literature with economics content" (p. 46). Kehler (1997) argued that teachers could continue to use the same children's literature they already in use in their classrooms as such literature "is replete with economic ideas that enable young people to relate their own experiences to their economic environment" (p. 26).

VanFossen (2003) described three arguments for using children's literature to teach economic concepts. First, literature is motivating for students. As Rodgers et al. (2007, p. 47) stated, "most children enjoy stories, [so] teaching economics within a literature framework can add to student motivation. The visual images and text work together to help students conceptualize how economics operates in the world around them."

Second, because it is motivational, children value the stories contained in quality literature all the more. Therefore, when these stories happen to contain economic concepts, students begin to see economics as part of the real world around them, and many children's stories deal with experiences that highlight children's role as participants in that economic world. Young children who read these stories also "develop comprehension of the difficult economic choices faced by their families" (Hendricks et al., 1986, p. 1).

Last, using children's literature to teach economics has a "positive externality." A positive externality is defined by economists as an unintended benefit associated with consumption or production. Teachers who use literature in their classroom are teaching both literacy and economics. Because the elementary school curriculum is already overcrowded—one where testing in math and reading often crowd out social studies instruction—integration means both economics and reading can be taught. Table 11.1 shows but a few of the dozens of pieces of quality literature that can be used to develop student understanding of economic concepts.

Using Internet-based lessons to teach elementary economics. In 1999, Henry Jay Becker wrote that "along with word processing, the Internet may be the most valuable of the many computer technologies available to teachers and students" (p. 32). A decade later, the Internet has become nearly ubiquitous in schools and classrooms. Numerous authors have written about the educational potential of the Internet for K–12 students. For example, Wilson (1995) wrote that, because of its interactive and multimedia nature, using the Internet in the classroom can break down the classroom's physical limitations and expand students' experiences (Wilson, 1995) and development of students' inquiry and analytical skills (Braun et al., 1997). What's more, Sosin and Becker (2000) have described a number of potential

Table 11.1 Sample Children's Literature

TITLE (AUTHOR)	PUBLISHER	ECONOMICS CONCEPTS
Anna the Bookbinder (Andrea Cheng)	Walker and Company (2003)	Goods and services, human capital
One Fine Day (Nonny Hogrogian)	Aladdin Paperbacks (1971)	Barter/exchange
If You Give a Mouse a Cookie (Laura Numeroff)	HarperCollins (1985)	Unlimited wants, goods and services
Grandpa's Corner Store (Dyanne DiSalvo-Ryan)	HarperCollins (2000)	Markets, competition, entrepreneurship
The Lorax (Dr. Seuss)	Random House (1971)	Scarcity, factors of production, productivity, long-run vs. short-run
Winnie's New Computer (Korky Paul and Valerie Thomas)	Oxford University (2003)	Capital goods
Pancakes, Pancakes (Eric Carle)	Aladdin Paperbacks (1998)	Productive resources, scarcity, opportunity costs, exchange

Source: Rodgers et al. (2007); VanFossen (2003).

benefits to using Internet-based teaching in economics classrooms at the pre-collegiate level.

However, a number of studies have found that most classroom teachers do not use Internet-based lessons in their classrooms. Becker (1999) found that only 25 percent of teachers in grades 4–12 used the Internet regularly in their classrooms. VanFossen and Waterson (2008) found that the vast majority of K–5 teachers in Indiana rarely, if ever, used Internet-based instruction with their students. The most common barriers to Internet use reported were: lack of training, and concern over developing effective Internet-based instruction.

The Council on Economic Education's *EconEdLink* addresses this last concern by providing K–5 teachers and students with more than 150 Internet-based lessons and classroom learning activities based on the *Voluntary National Content Standards in Economics* (Council for Economic Education, 1997). *EconEdLink* allows the user to employ several search strategies to find quality online lessons by economic concept as well as by grade level. For example, the *Quick Search* function allows the user to sort lessons by one or more of 50+ economic concepts. The *Featured Lessons* function generates results based on the most popular lessons at the site.

The *CyberTeach* section of *EconEdLink* provides additional Internet resources for teachers, including an economics calendar, a glossary, and additional reading. Teachers can also access real-time economic data on the Web. Finally, teachers can subscribe to the *EconEdLink* online newsletter, EconEdLetter (www.econedlink.org/cyberteach/econedletter.cfm), with access to updates about the site as well as descriptions of featured lessons.

One of the newest features of the *EconEdLink* site is the *MyEconEdLink* function. This feature lets users explore and save lessons based to a profile they create and to retrieve and use those lessons any time. *MyEconEdLink* can be set to identify individual state standards addressed by these saved lessons.

Using the Classroom Mini-Economy simulation. In 1983, Marilyn Kourilsky published the first commercially produced elementary classroom simulation on the economy at large. *Mini-Society* was a "very complex social simulation [which] engaged students in developing a classroom government, a classroom economic system, and other classroom social structures" (VanFossen, 2003, p. 93). While *Mini-Society* was very popular, many elementary teachers did not feel comfortable implementing the entire simulation. Of those who did, however, many "found success in implementing the classroom economy portion of the simulation" (VanFossen, 2003, p. 93).

Based in part on this success, authors created and published other simulations that focused exclusively on creating classroom economies. For example, the Indiana Department of Education published a version based on Kourilsky's classroom economy titled *The Classroom Mini-Economy: Integrating Economics into the Elementary and Middle School Curriculum* (Day et al., 1997). The *Classroom Mini-Economy* (CME) curriculum described a comprehensive, integrated curriculum in which students would learn economics by developing an economy in their own classroom. The CME curriculum laid out a series of steps for the teacher to follow:

1. Students develop a monetary system and design the classroom's currency.
2. Students (with teacher input) determine how they will earn classroom currency (e.g., jobs students will be paid for, goods they might create and sell, services they will provide).
3. Students (again with teacher input) determine what classroom currency can be spent on (e.g., items from a class store, class privileges, etc.).
4. Students determine how these privileges and items will distributed (e.g., running a class store, holding an auction, etc.).

Implementing a CME can still be quite daunting for an elementary teacher, especially one with only a limited economics background. Day et al. (1997) argued that the benefits associated with using a CME outweighed any such concerns. Among these benefits were that CME helps teach economic concepts in interesting ways, and thus improves student economic learning. In addition, CME can be easily integrated across the curriculum and thus can serve as a tremendous motivator. Finally, because CME offers an accurate simulation of our economy at large, students learn valuable lessons including how to manage their own money. Consider the following from a third-grade classroom teacher who implemented CME in her classroom:

> I have a difficult group of students this year. Many of them came in hating school. Mini-Economy is the one thing that we do where everyone is excited about learning. One boy said he can't sleep the night before we have Mini-Economy because he's so excited about all his ideas!! It doesn't get any better than that (Day et al., 1997, p. 11).

The *Mini-Economy* approach can be modified to match the appropriate developmental level of students. For example, teachers could run a CME as a simple token economy used primarily for classroom management. But CME could also be used to engage students in a much more sophisticated examination of how markets actually work. Some enterprising teachers have gone so far as charging students rent for their desks, levying taxes on student income, enforcing fines for environmental violations such as having a dirty classroom, and having student create real businesses that generate real class income.

Integrating economic concepts into other content areas. As noted earlier, high-stakes testing in math and reading are "crowding out" social studies in the K–5 curriculum (VanFossen and Waterson, 2008). This has made teaching economic content more challenging because the social studies have historically been the curricular home of economics in the elementary classroom. One way to address these challenges is to integrate economics concepts into content areas that continue to remain an integral part of the elementary curriculum. One such content area is mathematics.

According to the Council for Economic Education (2009),

> teaching mathematics in today's elementary classroom can be both exciting and challenging for an elementary teacher ... because we are experiencing a wonderful evolution in mathematics education that recognizes the importance of teaching mathematics in a hands-on, dynamic and applied way.

Weiss and Pasley (2004) found that teaching mathematics in an applied way can be an effective approach because integrating appropriate content (such as economics) influences student learning.

In addition, such an integrated approach provides meaningful, real-world applications of both economics and mathematical concepts. The authors concluded that student engagement and interaction with the content were factors associated with successful teaching.

One example of such integrated mathematics and economics curriculum is *Mathematics and Economics: Connections for Life (Grades 3–5)* (Council for Economic Education, 2009). This volume contains 12 lessons "designed by master teachers, reviewed by content experts, piloted in elementary classrooms and published with a careful attention to the potential excitement and utility of blending instruction" using mathematics and economics (Council on Economic Education, 2009, n.p.). One of these lessons is "Choices, Choices" which combines the use of a decision-making model (from economics) with data collection from surveys (mathematics). Students develop a survey about potential careers and use it to collect data. They then use the survey results and a decision-making grid to rank career choices and to create fractions in order to represent the survey data.

A second example is the lesson "Pizza on a Budget." This lesson combines the concept of budgeting and basic operations from mathematics such as addition, multiplication and estimating. The students generate a budget work sheet which they then use to plan a class pizza party. Other basic operations skills are reinforced during the lesson and students use decimals (during as discussion of money) to make decisions about refreshments for the party.

Using Financial Fitness for Life. Historically, neither personal finance education nor consumer economics has been part of the suggested content of economic education. However, recent events such as the housing market bubble, the sub-prime mortgage debacle, Americans' risky investments in securitized debt instruments, and the catastrophic events in the national and international financial sectors have led to a renewed chorus of economic educators calling for financial literacy to be front and center in economic education. This "chorus of advocates for more financial literacy grows louder everyday" (Morton, 2005, p. 66). Many who advocate for personal finance education claim that had American investors been better prepared, some or all of these debacles could have been avoided. No less an advocate than Federal Reserve Board Chairman Alan Greenspan joined this chorus stressing that economic education needed "to focus directly on providing youth with a foundation for understanding personal financial management" (2005, p. 64). Morton (2005) argued that personal finance content must be part of what constitutes economic literacy because "economics and personal finance are ultimately about choices and the consequences of those choices" (pp. 66–67).

It is important to start financial education early, in the elementary schools, so that students understand the processes of saving and investing. This will ultimately lead to making better decisions about managing their money—decisions that will impact them well into adulthood and beyond. The Council for Economic Education has developed a comprehensive curriculum called *Financial Fitness for Life* (FFFL). As its name suggests, the FFFL curriculum draws heavily on physical fitness analogies to introduce and teach financial literacy concepts. Each lesson, for example, is called a "workout" and each contains an introduction (a "warm-up") and a concluding activity (a "cool-down").

The curriculum for grades K–2, "Pocket Power," provides 16 lessons divided into five themes: (1) earning an income, (2) saving, (3) spending, (4) borrowing, and (5) managing money. All 16 lessons have "cross-training" activities that integrate language arts, music, mathematics, and technology in order to reinforce these key financial concepts. Most lessons come with CD-ROM-based multimedia activities. The lesson "A Very Good Day" has an animated slide show of a short story (with narration) that follows kids Penny and Nicholas as they learn about earning an income. Following the story, students participate in an interactive quiz on the key elements and financial concepts in the lesson.

In addition to the more than a dozen lessons at each grade-level cluster (K–2, 3–5, 6–8), the FFFL curriculum includes a supporting website that includes teaching suggestions and that provides additional web links to helpful resources. The K–2 website, for example, has more than a dozen examples of children's literature that contain key financial concepts and suggestions for making connections to math and language arts.

Conclusion

Young children can—and should—learn economics. If recent economic events have taught us anything it is that we cannot afford an economically illiterate population, and evidence clearly suggests that the place to start developing this economic literacy is early. Economics and economic understanding are too important to be left for coverage in the secondary school or the university. By then it is too late. Children live, and participate, in an economic world—they make decisions every single day. Economic education can help them develop into more systematic decision-makers, now and in the future. It is becoming increasingly important that educators use the best resources and the most promising teaching practices to help our next generation of citizens develop economic understanding. This chapter has developed a case for economic education in the elementary grades and has described several approaches for implementing economic education in the elementary curriculum. To conclude, it is important to reconsider Nobel Prize-winning economist James Tobin's (1986) rationale for the importance of developing economic literacy in which he argued that *all* citizens:

> will be making economic choices all their lives, as breadwinners and consumers, as citizens and voters. A wide range of people will bombard them with economic information and misinformation for their entire lives. They will need some capacity for critical judgment. They will need it whether they go on to college or not.

References

Agency for Instructional Technology. (1989). *Econ and me: Teacher's guide.* Bloomington, IN: Author.

Becker, H. (1999). *Internet use by teachers: Conditions of professional use and student-directed use* (Irvine, CA: Center for Research on Information Technology and Organizations); Retrieved on October 15, 2009 from: www.crito.uci.edu/TLC/findings/Internet-Use/startpage.htm.

Berti, A. (1988). *The child's construction of economics.* Oxford: Oxford University Press.

Berti, A. and Bombi, A. (1981). The development of money and its value: A longitudinal analysis. *Child Development,* 82, 1179–1182.

Braun, J., Fernlund, P., and White, C. (1998). *Technology tools in the social studies curriculum.* Wilsonville, OR: Franklin, Beedle and Assoc.

Council for Economic Education. (2009). *Mathematics and economics: Connections for life (grades 3–5)*. Retrieved on October 16, 2009 from: http://mathandecon.councilforeconed.org/35/intro.php.

Council for Economic Education. (1997). *Voluntary national content standards in economics*. Retrieved on October 19, 2009 from: www.councilforeconed.org/ea/program.php?pid=19.

Day, H., Foltz, M., Heyse, K., Marksbary, C., and Sturgeon, M. (1997). *Teaching economics using children's literature*. Indianapolis: Indiana Department of Education.

Diez-Martinez, E. and Ochoa, A. (2003). Mexican children's and adolescent's development of occupational hierarchy related to consumption and saving. *Children's Social and Economic Education*, 5 (3), 148–163.

Gallagher, S. (2010). Let's teach students to prioritise: Reconsidering needs vs. wants. *Social Studies and the Young Learner*, 22 (3), 14–16.

Greenspan, A. (2005). The importance of financial education today. *Social Education*, 69 (2), 64–65.

Greenspan, R. (2003). The kids are alright with spending. *ClickZ*. September 16, 2003. Retrieved on October 14, 2009 from: www.clickz.com/3077581.

Harrington, P. and Rueff, J. (2000). *Lawrence Senesh: His life and legacy*. West Lafayette, IN: Purdue University Press.

Harris Interactive (2000). *Results of Nickelodeon Online/Harris Interactive Kidpulse^sm and Mtv/Harris Interactive Youthpulse^sm studies*. Retrieved on October 15, 2009 from: www.harrisinteractive.com/news/index.asp?NewsID=143&HI_election=All.

Hendricks, R., Nappi, A., Dawson, G., and Mattila, M. (1986). *Learning economics through children's stories*. New York: Joint Council on Economic Education, 1986, p. 1.

Kehler, A. (1998). Capturing the "economic imagination": A treasury of children's books to meet content standards. *Social Studies and the Young Learner*, 11 (2), 26–29.

Kourilsky, M. (1993). Economic education and a generative model of mislearning and recovery. *Journal of Economic Education*, 24 (1), 23–33.

Kourilsky, M. (1983). *Mini-society: Experiencing real-world economics in the elementary school classroom*. Menlo Park, CA: Addison-Wesley.

Kourilsky. M. (1977). The kinder-economy: A case study of kindergarten pupils' acquisition of economic concepts. *The Elementary School Journal*, 77, 182–191.

Laney, J. (1993). Experiential versus experience-based learning and instruction. *Journal of Educational Research*, 86 (4), 228–236.

Laney, J. and Schug, M. (1998). Teach kids economics and they will learn. *Social Studies and the Young Learner*, 11 (2), 13–17.

Laney, J., Moseley, P., and Pak, L. (1996). Children's ideas about selected art and economic concepts before and after an integrated unit of instruction. *Children's Social and Economics Education*, 1 (1), 61–78.

Larkins, A. and Shaver, J. (1969). Economics learning in grade 1: The USU assessment studies. *Social Education*, 33 (1969), 955–963.

McNeal, J. (1999). *The kids market: Myths and realities*. Ithaca, NY: Paramount Market.

Meszaros, B. (2010). It's never too early: Why economics education in the elementary classroom. *Social Studies and the Young Learner*, 22 (3), 4–7.

Miller, S.L. and VanFossen, P.J. (2008). Recent research on the teaching and learning of pre-collegiate economics education. In L. Levstik and C. Tyson (Eds.), *Handbook of research in social studies education*. New York: Routledge, pp. 284–306.

Morton, J. (2005). The interdependence of economic and personal finance education. *Social Education*, 69 (2), 66–69.

Morgan, J. (1991). Using *Econ and Me* to teach economics to children in primary grades. *The Social Studies*, 82 195–197.

Robinson, H.F. (1963). *Learning economic concepts in the kindergarten*. Unpublished doctoral dissertation, Columbia University, New York. Retrieved October 13, 2009, from Dissertations and Theses: Full Text (Publication No. AAT 6305860).

Rodgers, Y., Hawthorne, S., and Wheeler, R. (2007). Teaching economics through children's literature in the primary grades. *The Reading Teacher*, 61 (1) 46–55.

Schug, M. (1994). How children learn economics. *International Journal of Social Education*, 8 (3), 25–34.

Schug, M. (1985). Introduction. In M.C. Schug (Ed.), *Economics in the school curriculum, K–12*. Washington, DC: National Council on Economic Education and the National Education Association.

Schug, M. and Birkey, C. (1985). The development of children's economic reasoning. *Theory and Research in Social Education*, 13 (1), 31–42.

Schug, M. and Lephardt, N. (1992). Development in children's thinking about international trade. *Social Studies*, 83.

Schug, M. and Walstad, W. (1991). Teaching and learning economics. In J. Shaver (Ed.), *Handbook of research on social studies teaching and learning*. New York: Macmillan Reference Books.

Senesh, L. (1964). *Our working world*. Chicago, IL: SRA.

Sosin, K. and Becker, W. (2000). Online teaching resources: A new journal section. *Journal of Economic Education*, 31 (1), 3–7.

Sosin, K., Dick, J., and Reiser, M. (1997). Determinants of achievement of economics concepts by elementary school students. *Journal of Economic Education*, 28 (Spring), 100–121.

Stern, G. (1999). Do we know enough about economics? *The Region*, 12, (4), 2–4.

Taba, H., Durkin, M., Fraenkel, J., and McNaughton, A. (1971). *Teachers' handbook to elementary social studies: An inductive approach* (2nd ed.). Reading, MA: Addison-Wesley.

Tobin, J. (1986). Economic literacy isn't a marginal issue, *Wall Street Journal.* July 9, 1986.

VanFossen, P.J. (2003). Best practice economic education for young children? It's elementary...! *Social Education*, 67 (2), 90–94.

VanFossen, P.J. and Waterson, R. (2008). "It's just easier to do what you did before...": An update on internet use in secondary social studies classrooms in Indiana. *Theory and Research in Social Education*, 36 (2), 124–152.

Watts, M. (2005). *What works: A review of research on outcomes and effective program delivery in precollege economic education.* New York: National Council on Economic Education.

Webley, P. and Plaisier, Z. (1998). Mental accounting in childhood. *Children's Social and Economic Education*, 3 (2), 55–64.

Weiss, I. and Pasley, J. (2004). What is high-quality instruction? *Educational Leadership*, 61 (5), 24–28.

Wilson, J. (1995). Social studies online resources. *Social Studies and the Young Learner*, 7 (3), 24–26.

12

WHAT RESEARCH TELLS US ABOUT TEACHING HIGH SCHOOL ECONOMICS

Michael Watts and William B. Walstad

Most of the contributions in this book have focused on contemporary issues facing economic educators. In this chapter, we will place the role of economic education in a historical context, stressing what research tells us about teaching economics at the high school level. We review the long-standing debate among economists about teaching economics at the precollege level. Should it be taught at all? Are high school teachers and students up to the challenge? How should it be taught? We then report on a recent extensive review of the research on outcomes and effective program delivery in precollege economic education.[1] We conclude by summarizing what we know and don't know about teaching economics in high school.

The Debate on Precollege Economic Education

The subjects of history and geography long dominated the social studies curriculum, closely followed by courses in civics or government. The emergence of economics as part of the "big four" is a more recent development. It might surprise some readers that prominent U.S. economists have long debated whether it makes sense to teach economics in U.S. high schools, let alone in earlier grades. Today some economists still claim that high school courses in economics are likely to do more harm than good (e.g., Colander, 2005; McCloskey, 2000).

Today's debates have their roots in the 1960s, when the American Economic Association directly addressed precollege economic education (National Task Force on Economic Education, 1961; Bach, 1967). Two key points made then, by authorities as prominent as

Nobel Laureate Paul Samuelson and distinguished economic educator Lee Bach, are still important today:

1. Young people are regularly exposed to misinformation about economic concepts and issues, which is very difficult and expensive to "unlearn" by the time they are in college classes; and
2. Most people never take a college course in economics, so waiting for college courses in economics to develop economic literacy "writes off" most of the population of future consumers, savers, investors, workers, and citizens.

On the other side of the argument, Nobel Laureate George Stigler took the lead. Although Stigler agreed there was a compelling case for economic education at the precollege level—because he recognized that people wanted to talk about money more than they wanted to talk about theology, music, or most other subjects (Stigler, 1970)—a key problem he saw facing general economic education was the profession not knowing how to teach basic economics effectively.

The Development of Standards and Curriculum

In the decades since the original debate, a series of curriculum guidelines for precollege economic education was published. A major example is the *National Voluntary Standards* document in economics (National Council on Economic Education, 1997)[2], which was developed at the time national standards documents were being published in most major academic disciplines, often with federal support and in response to issues identified in the 1983 report, *A Nation at Risk* (National Commission on Excellence in Education, 1983), and in subsequent legislation such as the No Child Left Behind Act (2001).

The standards document in economics identifies only 20 broad standards/generalizations for precollege economics; but the underlying economics content for each standard, identified in hundreds of content "benchmarks" that students are expected to understand by various grade levels, makes it clear that economics remains a challenging subject to teach even for well trained teachers and in schools with a comprehensive and well integrated curriculum in economics. And finding adequate time in the curriculum to teach economics, given competing demands from other subjects and educational initiatives, is a major challenge.

Today the share of high school students who take an economics course is nearly 50 percent (Walstad, 2001), in large part reflecting state and local school district graduation requirements. The requirements vary widely but the typical course lasts for one semester.[3] As the market for the high school economics course grew over these decades, so too did initiatives to include economics instruction in other social studies courses, and particularly in elementary grades even in core subjects such as language arts, mathematics, and science (where policy issues related to environmental economics and health care are regularly covered). The adoption of formal standards in most subject areas in many cases led to an increase in the demand for infusion or multidisciplinary education including economics. Certainly standards developed by the national organizations in other academic disciplines, and particularly other social studies areas, explicitly included a considerable amount of economics.[4] But in practice the national discipline-based standards documents have had less direct impact on classroom practice than the comprehensive state standards covering all major subject areas. These were usually developed working with the national discipline standards documents but generally did not—and given classroom time constraints almost certainly could not—adopt all of the content recommended in all of the discipline-specific standards. In most cases the state standards are backed up with annual standardized testing of students in key grade levels, and in some states that includes test items on economics. But there is considerable variance in the standards and testing programs adopted across the states, and there is some well publicized evidence that subjects that are not included in state standards and assessments are "crowded out" of the curriculum and classroom (Toppo, 2007). In many states that includes economics.

The increase in the demand has led to a second major change since the 1960s: a remarkable increase in the number and range of textbooks and supplementary materials dealing with economics. Today many of the instructional materials for precollege economics—especially the supplementary materials—feature student-centered and active-learning teaching methods. These materials have been developed not only by commercial publishers but also by non-profit groups such as the Council for Economic Education, Junior Achievement, and Federal Reserve banks. Corporations and corporate foundations (for example, McDonalds, Procter and Gamble, and the Amoco Foundation) have also supported the development and dissemination of films or extensive packets of lessons on economics for use at the pre-college level, as have labor studies programs, environmental groups, financial and consumer education organizations and coalitions, and a wide range of other special interest groups.

Key Findings from Research on Precollege Economic Education

Studies of precollege economic education have identified three key factors that influence how much economics students learn in U.S. schools: (1) the amount of time students spend on economics in their classes, (2) teachers' knowledge and training in economics, and (3) the use of instructional materials with good economics content and pedagogical methods that students and teachers find interesting and accessible.

Amount of Time Students Spend Learning Economics

There are many studies showing that secondary and even elementary students can learn basic concepts and discuss applications and issues from economics. Moreover, as the amount of classroom time spent teaching economics increases, students learn more. The gains from additional instructional time are quite possibly more evident for economics (and other subjects not taught at all grade levels, or rarely taught as a separate course for more than one semester) than might be found in core subjects such as mathematics, English, and science. The level of student achievement in economics, even in the high school course, is generally not nearly as high as economists and economic educators would like it to be (Walstad and Buckles, 2008; Walstad, 2001), but the same point has been made about undergraduate principles courses, too, as noted earlier by Stigler (1963) and in recent studies (Walstad and Allgood, 1999; Walstad and Rebeck, 2008).

Most of the studies in economics have relied on nationally normed, standardized multiple-choice tests, or modified versions of these tests. The very few studies that look at similar kinds of long-term effects for precollege education programs have dealt mainly with the effects of curriculum mandates in the area of personal finance. For example, Bernheim et al. (2001) found that students who attended high school in states with mandates on financial education reported being exposed to more financial education, with the level of exposure increasing steadily over time after the mandates were adopted. The authors also report on changes in financial behavior that may be related to financial education. Adults who attended high school in states with financial education mandates saved significantly more than those who attended high school in states without mandated courses. In addition, net wealth was significantly higher for students who graduated after the mandates took effect. Tennyson and Nguyen (2001) found that students in states that required specific financial education course work scored significantly higher on a test of personal financial literacy than students in states with no mandates or with only a broadly worded and general mandate for providing financial education.

The most reliable way to get a large increase in student understanding of economics is through a separate semester- or year-long course in economics. Even without a separate course, there is an important and in some ways inescapable role for infusion approaches that entail teaching economics in other subject areas. First, a single course in economics (or any other subject) is unlikely to make students literate in any meaningful or lasting sense. Second, economic concepts and issues are inevitably addressed in many other academic subjects, including history, civics, and most social studies courses, so the question is not really whether but instead how effectively economics will be taught in those courses. The U.S. experience has repeatedly shown that infusion of economics in a wide range of grade levels and subject areas can be done, but that it is difficult to implement effectively and even harder to sustain. Part of the sustainability problem is the long-standing pattern of faddishness in educational practices and reforms, so that what captures the interest of educators and policy-makers today is likely to fade and be replaced by something new in a few years. But it is inherently difficult and expensive to train teachers to infuse content across multiple subject areas and grade levels, to coordinate and sequence that instruction effectively, and to develop sound instructional materials that are truly interdisciplinary.

Teachers' Knowledge and Training in Economics

The second key finding from studies on precollege economic education concerns the effects of teachers' training in the content and teaching of economics. Teachers at these grade levels have completed low average levels of coursework in economics (Bosshardt and Watts, 2005), but there is considerable variance, too, and when students are taught economics by teachers who know more economics, students reliably learn more economics. That result appears in general studies on instructor effects for teachers at the high school, middle school, and intermediate grade levels (Bosshardt and Watts, 1990, 1994); in studies based on national samples using standardized tests at these grade levels (Allgood and Walstad, 1999; Walstad, 1992) and in studies on the use of a wide range of instructional materials.

The Use of Instructional Materials

The first finding—or perhaps non-finding—to note about instructional materials in precollege economics is that to date no particular pedagogical approach or instructional media format (film, DVDs, computers, games or simulations, role plays, and so forth) has been found to be consistently superior in improving student performance, or even superior to standard "chalk and talk" presentations by classroom teachers.[5] Becker et al. (1990) reached that conclusion in a review of research on precollege economic education 20 years ago, and as a general finding it still holds. Some teachers and education professors may find that surprising, because in the general education literature there have been widespread claims about the advantages of active-learning methods. But Becker (2004, p. 265) points out that a very small number and share of the published studies on active learning or on classroom assessment techniques have been quantitative studies employing inferential statistics. It is still possible, of course, that in the future some new pedagogical method or technology, or a revised version of existing methods and technologies, may prove to be superior to other approaches. Until then such standbys as the Socratic Method and chalk and talk lectures are likely to remain with us, doing relatively little harm to student learning, on average, even if most students find other approaches more interesting and enjoyable.

Even without compelling evidence of one dominant method for teaching economics in precollege economic education, there are now examples of many different kinds of instructional approaches and technologies working effectively—compared to standard levels of achievement in courses at different age and grade levels. Bach and Saunders (1965) found that a year-long television series sponsored by the AEA in 1961, carried by over 182 CBS affiliate stations and then by nearly all U.S. educational television stations in 1962–1963, raised scores for teachers and students who received academic credit for watching the programs and completing exams by about as much as a year-long undergraduate course in economics. In the 1980s, many different film series for precollege economic education were nationally distributed—first in 16 mm format and later as videotapes—and often shown on educational television stations. Studies found these film series to be effective in raising student scores on standardized tests (for example, see Chizmar et al., 1985; Walstad, 1980).

By the 1990s, computer software and DVD programs largely supplanted film series, taking advantage of lower production costs and the rapid spread of computers into U.S. classrooms. These formats are often better suited for use by individual students at computer workstations rather than being shown to an entire class. They are therefore more likely to be used as supplementary materials, often as enhancement or extension activities for individual students. In economics most materials in these formats have been produced by small, independent producers, with lower budgets and production values than the national film series, and usually no budget at all for supporting evaluation and assessment work.

There has been a resurgence in the number and range of print materials issued by commercial and non-profit publishers. These formats also are less likely to be the subject of formal research and assessment studies, but a federally funded program to train the trainers of economics teachers in transition and developing nations, featuring an extensive set of print materials published by the Council on Economic Education (formerly known as the National Council on Economic Education), has been the subject of several published and ongoing studies (for example, Scahill, 2006; Walstad, 2002; Walstad and Rebeck, 2001). These studies have confirmed the key role of teacher training and use of the instructional materials provided to participants in the programs, with materials translated and adapted to reflect different institutional features and local examples in other countries. Many of these lessons feature classroom simulations, cooperative learning, and alternative pedagogical strategies. These methods may not increase student learning compared to other lesson formats that receive the same amount of class time, but nevertheless may be more interesting and comfortable for both students and pre-college teachers to use.

What We Know and What We Don't Know

After several years of research in economic education, we can say a few things for sure. First, young people can learn economics. Students learn more as the amount of classroom time spent teaching economics increases. This is true at both the secondary and elementary levels. While there are many important reasons to want to integrate economics throughout social studies and other parts of the curriculum, it remains true that the most reliable way to get a large increase in student understanding of economics is through a separate semester- or year-long course in economics. Second, teachers who know more economics can teach it more effectively to their students than do teachers who know less economics. Finally, while there has been a sea change in the quantity of materials available for teaching economics, there is no compelling evidence that one dominant teaching method is superior to the others.

There is, of course, a lot we do not know about teaching economics. One debate that is very much on the table is: How much economics can reasonably be taught in high schools, middle schools, and elementary schools? What concepts and understandings are most important for students who will not take any economics beyond the one-semester high school course, or for students who will not even take that course? Stigler felt that college principles classes, which he described as "introductory-terminal" courses (1963, p. 658) for most students, were covering far too much material, and too much technical and textbook material on definitions, diagrams, and techniques, rather than focusing on economic problems. The high school economics class today is usually taught as a cut-down version of a one-semester college survey course on microeconomics and macroeconomics. We know students can learn at least some of that material in the high school class, and for the past two decades very bright and motivated high school students have even done well in Advanced Placement courses in economics, using standard college textbooks (Melican et al., 1997). But it would still be interesting to see how different kinds of courses, such as the kind of course Stigler proposed, would affect student learning and retention.

What are the long-term effects of learning economics? As we mentioned earlier, one study suggests that students who take mandated courses in personal finance have higher savings rates and more wealth. How might courses in economics influence the behavior of consumers, workers, and voters?

The number of states requiring a high school economics course to be taken for graduation has increased to 21 in 2009 from 13 in 1998 (Council on Economic Education, 2009). These mandated states include states with large school enrollments such as California, Florida, New York, and Texas. Are these requirements effective? Common sense suggests that the answer is "yes." Recall, however, that nearly every high school in the nation requires students to complete a two-semester course in U.S. history for graduation. Yet, the National Assessment of Educational Progress (NAEP) reports consistently low levels of achievement in student historical understanding (U.S. Department of Education, 2006). Thus, it is a serious question regarding how effective state mandates are in social studies in general and economics in particular. Comparing basic measures of student achievement in economics in states that require a high school economics course to those that do not would be a worthwhile contribution to the discussion about the desirability of those course requirements.

A significant development for economic education in the schools in recent years was the NAEP in economics (Walstad and Buckles, 2008). NAEP testing has been conducted in major subjects in the school curriculum for decades including history, civics, and geography. In 2006 the first NAEP test in economics was administered to a nationally representative sample of over 11,000 twelfth-grade students. This testing is further recognition that economics has become an important part of the school curriculum. NAEP uses a content framework (NAGB, 2006) based on the national standards in economics, divided into three categories: market economy (microeconomics); national economy (macroeconomics); and international economy. The results show there are significant gaps in high school students' understanding of many basic economic concepts (Mead and Sandene, 2007). For example, students had problems with test items asking them to identify a tool of monetary policy, explain how a change in the cost to produce a product will influence its price, or determine the effect of changes in exchange rates on exports or imports. In 2012 the NAEP economics test will be administered again, providing a measure of changes in student achievement over time. The NAEP data for economics will become an increasingly important resource for monitoring the economics achievement of high school students and for investigations of these research questions.

We have far more information about precollege economic education today than when this work began 50 years ago. That helps to provide better answers to some of the questions raised in those debates, but there are certainly many key questions that remain, as well as new questions raised, by changing public policies and educational environments.

Notes

1. Watts (2006), available online from the Council for Economic Education (www.councilforeconomiced.org). The chapter in the report reviewing research on precollege economic education was coauthored by Walstad. The report also includes a chapter on long-term effects and outcomes of economic education that is briefly discussed in this chapter, and several chapters on topics not discussed here due to space constraints, including related research from the fields of social studies education, business and vocational education, domain-specific education, and "expert-novice" studies.

2. The name of the National Council on Economic Education was changed to the Council on Economic Education in 2009. A revision of the *Standards* is to be published in 2010 (see www.councilforeconed.org).

3. For a recent listing of state requirements, see the "Survey of the States" (Council for Economic Education, 2009).

4. See Buckles and Watts (1998) for a review of the substantial but often flawed economics content included in the national standards for history, civics/government, social studies, and geography.

5. Addressing undergraduate teaching in economics, Bartlett (2006) reviews the literature on cooperative learning methods and concludes that there are generally gains in student learning, especially in small classes. Shanahan and Bredon (2006) report mixed and generally negative results in a review of the research on distance-learning programs. In one of the most comprehensive studies to date on the use of classroom experiments in economics classes, Emerson and Taylor (2004) find gains in student learning.

References

Allgood, S. and Walstad, W. B. (1999). The longitudinal effects of economic education on teachers and their students. *Journal of Economic Education, 30*(2), 99–111.

Bach, G.L. (1967). The state of education in economics. In K.G. Lumsden (Ed.), *New developments in the teaching of economics* (pp. 16–26). Englewood Cliffs, NJ: Prentice Hall.

Bach, G.L. and Saunders, P. (1965). Economic education: Aspirations and achievements. *American Economic Review, 55*(June), 329–356.

Bartlett, R.L. (2006). The evolution of cooperative learning and economics instruction. In W.E. Becker, M. Watts, and S.R. Becker (Eds.), *Teaching economics: More alternatives to chalk and talk* (pp. 39–58). Cheltenham, UK, and Northampton, MA: Edward Elgar.

Becker, W.E. (2004). Quantitative research on teaching methods in tertiary education. In W.E. Becker and M.L. Andrews (Eds.), *The scholarship of teaching and learning in higher education* (pp. 263–309). Bloomington, IN: Indiana University Press.

Becker, W.E., Greene, W., and Rosen, S. (1990). Research on high school economic education. *Journal of Economic Education, 21*(3), 231–245.

Bernheim, B.D., Garrett, D.M., and Maki, D.M. (2001). Education and saving: The long-term effects of high school financial curriculum mandates. *Journal of Public Economics, 80*(June), 435–465.

Bosshardt, W. and Watts, M. (1990). Instructor effects and their determinants in precollege economic education. *Journal of Economic Education, 21*(3), 265–276.

Bosshardt, W. and Watts, M. (1994). Instructor effects in economics in elementary and junior high schools. *Journal of Economic Education, 25*(3), 195–211.

Bosshardt, W. and Watts, M. (2005). Teachers' undergraduate coursework in economics in the Baccalaureate and Beyond longitudinal study. *Journal of Economic Education, 36*(4), 400–406.

Buckles, S. and Watts, M. (1998). National standards in economics, history, social studies, civics, and geography: Complementarities, competition, or peaceful coexistence? *Journal of Economic Education, 29*(Spring), 157–166.

Chizmar, J.F., McCartney, B.J., Halinski, R.S., and Rachich, M.J. (1985). "Give and Take," economics achievement, and basic skills development. *Journal of Economic Education, 16*(1), 99–110.

Colander, D. (2005). What we teach and what we do. *Journal of Economic Education, 36*(3), 249–260.

Council for Economic Education. (2009). *Survey of the states 2009: The state of economic, financial and entrepreneurship education in our nation's schools.* Retrieved from: www.councilforeconed.org/about/survey2009.

Emerson, T.L.N. and Taylor, B.A. (2004). Comparing student achievement across experimental and lecture-oriented sections of a principles of microeconomics class. *Southern Economic Journal, 70*(3), 672–693.

McCloskey, D.N. (2000). Why economics should not be taught in high school. In D.N. McCloskey, *How to be human—Though an economist* (pp. 182–186). Ann Arbor, MI: University of Michigan Press.

Mead, N. and Sandene, B. (2007). *The nation's report card: Economics 2006* (NCES 2007-475). Washington, DC: National Center for Education Statistics, Institute of Education Sciences, U.S. Department of Education.

Melican, C., Debebe, F., and Morgan, R. (1997). Comparing AP and college student learning of economics. *Journal of Economic Education, 28*(2), 135–142.

National Assessment Governing Board (NAGB), U.S. Department of Education. (2006). *Economics framework for the 2006 national assessment of educational progress.* Retrieved from: www.nagb.org/publications/frameworks/economics_06.pdf.

National Commission on Excellence in Education. (1983, April). *A nation at risk: The imperative for educational reform.* Retrieved from: http://www2.ed.gov/pubs/NatAtRisk/index.html.

National Council on Economic Education. (1997). *Voluntary national content standards in economics.* New York: National Council on Economic Education.

National Task Force on Economic Education. (1961). *Economic education in the schools.* New York: Committee for Economic Development.

No Child Left Behind Act, 20 U.S.C. § 6319 (2001).

Scahill, E. (2006). Evaluation of the *Training of Trainers* programme: What did trainers know? What did they learn? *International Review of Economics Education, 5*(2), 9–28.

Shanahan, M. and Bredon, G. (2006). Teaching and learning economics at a distance. In W.E. Becker, M. Watts, and S.R. Becker (Eds.), *Teaching economics: More alternatives to chalk and talk* (pp. 39–58). Cheltenham, UK, and Northampton, MA: Edward Elgar.

Stigler, G.J. (1963). Elementary economic education. *American Economic Review, 53*(May), 657–659.

Stigler, G.J. (1970). The case, if any, for economic education. *Journal of Economic Education, 1*(Spring), 77–84.

Tennyson, S. and Nguyen, C. (2001). State curriculum mandates and student knowledge of personal finance. *Journal of Consumer Affairs, 35*(2), 241–262.

Toppo, G. (2007, January 8). How Bush education law has changed our nation's schools. *USA Today*, 1A–2A.

U.S. Department of Education. (2006). *The nation's report card: U.S. history 2006*. Washington, DC.

Walstad, W.B. (1980). The impact of "Trade-offs" and teacher training on economic understanding and attitudes. *Journal of Economic Education, 12*(1), 41–48.

Walstad, W.B. (1992). Economics instruction in high schools. *Journal of Economic Literature, 30*(December), 2019–2051.

Walstad, W.B. (2001). Economic education in U.S. high schools. *Journal of Economic Perspectives, 15*(3), 195–210.

Walstad, W.B. (2002). The effects of teacher programs on student economic understanding and market attitudes in transition economies. In M. Watts and W.B. Walstad (Eds.), *Reforming economics and economics teaching in the transition economies: From Marx to markets in the classroom* (pp. 63–96). Cheltenham, UK, and Northampton, MA: Edward Elgar.

Walstad, W.B. and Allgood, S. (1999). What do college seniors know about economics? *American Economic Review, 89*(2) (May), 350–354.

Walstad, W.B. and Buckles, S. (2008). The National Assessment of Educational Progress in Economics: Findings from general economics. *American Economic Review, 98*(2), 541–546.

Walstad, W.B. and Rebeck, K. (2001). Teacher and student understanding in transition economies. *Journal of Economic Education, 32*(1), 58–67.

Walstad, W.B., and Rebeck, K. (2008). The test of understanding of college economics. *American Economic Review, 98*(2), 547–551.

Watts, M. (2006). *What works: A review of research on outcomes and effective program delivery in precollege economic education*. New York: National Council on Economic Education. Retrieved from: www.council-foreconed.org/eee/research/WhatWorks.pdf.

Contributors

J.R. Clark earned the Ph.D. in Economics from Virginia Polytechnic Institute under the Nobel Laureate James Buchanan. He holds the Probasco Chair at the University of Tennessee at Chattanooga, and is the author of six books and numerous academic articles published in the United States, Austria, Japan, Italy, Canada, France, India, and Russia. Prior to coming to UTC, Professor Clark was with the Joint Council on Economic Education in New York, chaired a large university economics department in New Jersey, held the Hendrix Chair at UT Martin, and was a research fellow at Princeton University. In 1996, he was inducted into the Mont Pelerin Society and elected to its board of directors in 2006. Currently, he serves as Secretary/Treasurer for the Association of Private Enterprise Education and the Southern Economic Association, as well as a board member of Kenco Corp.

Lucien Ellington is UC Foundation Professor of Education and Co-director of the Asia Program at the University of Tennessee at Chattanooga. Professor Ellington is also a Senior Fellow with the Foreign Policy Research Institute and is the founding and current editor of the Association for Asian Studies teaching journal, *Education about Asia*. His publications include books, journal articles, and book chapters on Japan, economic education, economic and world history, and educational reform. Professor Ellington has also served as editor for two book series on Asia.

Barbara Flowers recently joined the Federal Reserve Bank of St. Louis as a senior economic education specialist. Prior to joining the Fed, she served as director of the Center for Entrepreneurship and Economic Education at the University of Missouri–St. Louis where she taught economics and developed curriculum in economics and personal finance. While at the center, she also developed the American Dream Youthpreneurship Program for high school students. She is the co-author of *Financial Fitness for Life, Grades*

6–8: Economics at Work, and elementary curriculum units, *Focus on Economics: K–2 and 3–5*, among others.

Selena Garrison is State Training Coordinator and Head Trainer of the Florida Master Money Mentor Program through the Department of Family, Youth, and Community Sciences, in the Institute for Food and Agricultural Sciences at the University of Florida. She holds B.Sc. degrees in both Psychology and Family, Youth, and Community Sciences from the University of Florida. She also holds a M.Sc. in Family, Youth, and Community Sciences from the University of Florida with a specialization in Family Financial Management. Her research interests focus on the impacts of financial socialization in relation to financial knowledge, attitudes, and behaviors. Her master's thesis focused on gender differences in financial socialization and willingness to take financial risks.

Michael S. Gutter is an Assistant Professor and Financial Management State Specialist for the Department of Family, Youth, and Community Sciences, in the Institute for Food and Agricultural Sciences at the University of Florida. His Ph.D. is in Family Resource Management from the Ohio State University with a specialization in Finance. The common theme that connects Gutter's research, teaching and outreach is helping households achieve financial security. His outreach projects include Managing in Tough Times, Florida Saves, Florida Master Money Mentor, and Get Checking. Professor Gutter is the current Vice President of the Florida Jump$tart Coalition and serves on the editorial boards for the *Journal of Consumer Affairs, Journal of Consumer Education*, and the *Journal of Financial Counseling and Planning*. His research and outreach has funding from Great Lakes Higher Education Guaranty Corporation, Bank of America, National Endowment for Financial Education, and the FINRA Investor Education Foundation.

James Gwartney holds the Gus A. Stavros Eminent Scholar Chair at Florida State University, where he directs the Stavros Center for the Advancement of Free Enterprise and Economic Education. He is the coauthor of *Economics: Private and Public Choice* (Cengage South-Western Press, 2010), a widely used principles of economics text that is now in its thirteenth edition. He is also the coauthor of the annual report, *Economic Freedom of the World*, which provides information on the consistency of institutions and policies with economic freedom for 141 countries. His publications have appeared in scholarly journals, including the *American Economic Review*, *Journal of Political Economy*, *Southern Economic Journal*, *Kyklos*, and *Journal of Institutional and Theoretical Economics*. During 1999–2000, he served as Chief Economist of the Joint Economic Committee of the U.S. Congress. He is a past President of the Southern Economic Association and the Association of Private Enterprise Education. His Ph.D. in economics is from the University of Washington.

Dwight R. Lee received his Ph.D. from the University of California, San Diego in 1972. Since that time he has had full-time tenured faculty appointments at the University of Colorado, Virginia Tech University, George Mason University, and the University of Georgia where he was the Ramsey Professor of Economics and Private Enterprise from 1985 to 2008. He is currently the William J. O'Neil Professor of Global Markets and Freedom at Southern Methodist University in Dallas. Professor Lee's research has covered a variety of areas, including the Economics of the Environment and Natural Resources, the Economics of Political Decision Making, Public Finance, Law and Economics, and Labor Economics. He was president of the Association of Private Enterprise Education for 1994–1995 and President of the Southern Economic Association from 1997 to 1998.

Jane S. Lopus is Professor of Economics and Director of the Center for Economic Education at California State University, East Bay. She holds a Ph.D. in Economics from the University of California, Davis and an undergraduate degree in political science from the University of Michigan, Ann Arbor. Professor Lopus teaches a wide variety of economics courses at Cal State East Bay and was named the University's Outstanding Professor in 2006. She is an active researcher in economic education and has won both research and leadership awards from the National Association of Economic Educators. As a former high school economics teacher, she has written many materials for teaching economics at the high school level. She is actively involved in the international programs of the Council on Economic Education.

John Morton is the Senior Program Officer for the Arizona Council on Economic Education. Previously, he was an economics teacher at Homewood-Flossmoor High School (Illinois), founder and director of the Governors State University Center for Economic Education (Illinois), founder and President of the Arizona Council on Economic Education, and Vice President for program development at the National Council on Economic Education. He chaired the advisory board of *The Wall Street Journal Classroom Edition* and has written 40 publications and books of instructional activities for the high school economics course, including four widely used textbooks.

M. Scott Niederjohn is Charlotte and Walter Kohler Professor of Economics at Lakeland College in Sheboygan, Wisconsin. He is also the Director of Lakeland's Center for Economic Education. Dr Niederjohn holds undergraduate and master's degrees from Marquette University and a Ph.D. in economics from the University of Wisconsin – Milwaukee. He has published more than 50 articles, monographs, reports, and curriculum materials in journals such as *Applied Economics, Monthly Labor Review, Journal of Urban Affairs, Eastern Economics Journal, Journal of Private Enterprise*, and *Wisconsin Interest*. His research is concentrated in the areas of economic education, public policy analysis, and applied microeconomics. Under his direction, the Lakeland College Center for Economic Education recently received a national award for the best new center in the United States.

Mark C. Schug is Professor Emeritus at the University of Wisconsin–Milwaukee. Professor Schug taught for 36 years at the middle school, high school, and university levels. He currently is a full-time consultant on economic and financial education and education policy. A widely recognized scholar, he has written and edited over 200 articles, books, and national curriculum materials. He served for three years as Senior Fellow with the Council on Economic Education. He serves on the boards of the Association of Private Enterprise, Business and Economics Academy of Milwaukee, Economics Wisconsin, University School of Milwaukee, the Governor's Council on Financial Literacy, and School Choice Wisconsin.

Angela M. Smith is an Assistant Professor of Economics at James Madison University. She holds a Ph.D. in economics from the University of Virginia with concentrations in public economics and industrial organization and a B.A. in economics from the College of William and Mary. Her primary research field is experimental economics and she has written multiple refereed articles in this area that examine various phenomena including exclusive contracts, security investments, individual probability updating, and firm product ordering behavior. She also uses experiments in the classroom to guide students to realize and understand economic concepts through experience.

Phillip J. VanFossen is the James F. Ackerman Professor of Social Studies Education, Director of the Ackerman Center for Democratic Citizenship, and Associate Director of the Purdue University Center for Economic Education at Purdue University. He holds a courtesy appointment in the Krannert School of Management at Purdue where he teaches introductory economics courses. He is the program author for a recently released high school economics textbook *Econ Alive!: The Power to Choose* (Teacher's Curriculum Institute, 2009). In addition to economic education, his research interests include the use of digital technology in social studies classrooms. He has authored three books, numerous chapters, and more than 25 refereed articles on these topics.

William B. Walstad is John T. and Mable M. Hay Professor of Economics at the University of Nebraska–Lincoln and Editor of the *Journal of Economic Education*. He is an expert on testing and assessment in economics. He served on the test committee for the 2006 National Assessment of Educational Progress (NAEP) in economics and now serves on the test committee for 2012 administration of NAEP economics. He helped construct the National Financial Capability Challenge test for the U.S. Department of the Treasury. He has directed projects to prepare many precollege tests, including the *Test of Economic Literacy* (high school), *Test of Economic Knowledge* (middle school), *Basic Economics Test* (elementary), and three *Financial Fitness for Life* tests (elementary, middle, and high school).

Michael Watts is a Professor of Economics and the director of the Center for Economic Education at Purdue University. He has served as President of the National Association of Economic Educators and the Society of Economics Educators, as Vice President of the Midwest Economic Association, and as a member and Chair of the American Economic Association's Committee on Economic Education. His main teaching interests include microeconomics, labor economics, and the history of economic thought. His major publications include *The Literary Book of Economics*, "Teachers' Undergraduate Coursework in Economics in the Baccalaureate and Beyond Longitudinal Study" (with W. Bosshardt), and "Instructor Effects and Their Determinants in Pre-College Economic Education" (with W. Bosshardt). He was a member of the writing team for the first edition of the voluntary national standards in economics. He has served as a consultant for such organizations as the Council on Economic Education, Agency for Instructional Technology, The College Board, the IMF, the U.S. Information Agency, and Microsoft.

William C. Wood is Professor of Economics and Director of the Center for Economic Education at James Madison University. An accomplished teacher and writer, Wood was the recipient of teaching awards at the University of Virginia and at James Madison University, where he was the 2001–2002 Distinguished Teacher in the College of Business. Wood was named in 2002 as an inaugural winner of the Southern Economic Association's Kenneth G. Elzinga Distinguished Teaching Award. Wood is also a past recipient of the Alpha Kappa Psi–Clifford D. Spangler award for research in risk and insurance and Best Paper award for the *Journal of Private Enterprise*. He is the author of three books, more than 30 scholarly articles, and national economic education materials for school and adult audiences.

Index

Note: Page numbers in *italics* denote tables, those in **bold** denote figures.